ROCK HOPPING
TALES OF A
SINGLE GRANNY

BOOK ONE – MOVING TO MALTA

For my Grandsons

TABLE OF CONTENTS

INTRODUCTION

As I approach my 60th Birthday, I find myself FINALLY at a place in life, where I can decide to change it enough by emigrating. No ties, or responsibilities, other than to myself and my numerous possessions. Done the married thing, am the mother, grandmother, sister, Godmother, friend, but none of the aforementioned are any prevention on my intentions. I am a happy free agent.

This is the story of what I decided to do about changing my circumstances and how I packed up all my belongings and started a new life in Malta, or Gozo to be more specific. It's difficult to sing your own praises about a book you've written, but I think this will be an enjoyable and rather funny read for anyone. I will show you how anyone can do this if they want to and if your plan is moving to Malta, or even having a holiday there, then this is certainly a <u>must</u> read. Most of it is written in a Diary format, as the preparation to leave the UK, the initial holiday to check the country out and then the actual arrival to live, are documented in an informative and amusing way. It's full of information about the islands and will be the best travel guide for Malta and Gozo that you could wish for. Most of all, I hope you enjoy the story about my new life and the first book in my rock hopping tales as a single Granny.

Islands have their own sleepy way of life and small island people are chilled out, generous and kind. Things will get done, but there's always something more important first – it takes a bit more time!

Looking into the logistics of a new Mediterranean life, there were certain things that were important to me. The first was the language issue – I didn't really want to have to learn a new one. In Malta 90% of the population speak fluent English. It's their second language and even when talking to each other, they switch between Maltese and English frequently. The children all grow up bi-lingual. The health care is very good – far better in fact than many areas in the UK. You can see a Doctor for free, if you want to spend time waiting at a clinic, or you can see a private Doctor with an appointment time, for €12 to €15 and you will get to spend half an hour or more with that Doctor if you need to. There are excellent hospitals, including one on Gozo and there's no shortage of specialist Consultants or Surgeons. This was an important issue for someone just turning 60! The EU reciprocal health care system meant that I didn't have to pay for hospital or outpatient care. The healthcare was something important to me when deciding to move there and also the fact that they drive on the same side of the road as the Brits and have a Lidl and a Waitrose!

I will find myself in three short months, sitting in Malta somewhere wonderful, a few days before my 60th birthday, knowing that I have come to the place where I'm going to live for as long as I want to. Since I now know with every instinct of my Being that I'm meant to go there, I will by that time, be mostly packed, with a monumental administrative task perhaps halfway done and will have a final four to six weeks left after my return to finish packing, more admin, selling the car, plus anything I don't want to store and ship. I'm hopping off this rock for the foreseeable future, or perhaps forever and it feels good!

The third 'sign' I was given about Malta came after three or four months of rather boring stability, life-wise, yet huge restlessness and lack of joy or enthusiasm in my heart. I can see quite clearly now that my inner being/heart/God part, wanted to move on, but the 'me' in my physical life had completely forgotten. Except I realised that I'd got to the point of actually looking forward to death, moving to the next dimension and was so bored I felt something just had to change. I knew that feeling like this is not what I was born to be feeling and that something very significant was missing. I needed guidance. One night in bed, after turning off the light, I decided to tell God that I didn't want to spend the rest of my physical form life sitting about waiting to come home and said I'm not sure what I'm meant to be doing. I prayed for guidance and my heart was in sorrow and low frequency and I was in tears.

Malta came into my head that night in a way that could never have not been noticed. I then remembered the first and second time I had been prompted about Malta, the second time being several years ago, when I was planning a holiday there, which never came to fruition, but as a consequence I had two guide books. Malta being shown to me very clearly for the third time got me so excited, I got out of bed and immediately grabbed the guide books and spent the rest of that night on line, investigating all Malta. I needed no caffeine, but I was buzzing!

The first time Malta kind of registered in my subconscious was a little more significant in the greater scheme of my life, of which at the time, I had no idea. I suppose in that moment it was as a sort of dreamy possibility that was a silent desire, back in September, 2010. My husband and I were with a couple who were our best friends and staying with us for the weekend. We were attending a Black Tie Ball and I was chatting to another friend of ours in general conversation and he mentioned Malta. I can't even remember what he said, it was just that it registered with me in a way I didn't realise until I was shown Malta for the third time, how significant the first time was. A month after that Black Tie Ball, I asked my husband of twenty years for a divorce. I didn't find out until a year or so later, that on that

Black Tie evening, my husband, when dancing with our best friend, apparently told her for the first time that he'd fallen in love with her. They are now living happily ever after and the significance of that little word Malta that night, is perhaps now guiding me to my happily ever after.

PREPARATION

I'm exceedingly thankful I've kept most of the boxes and bubble wrap from my move after the sale of our marital home, plus boxes and bubble wrap from my brothers move, so I have plenty of packing material. My organisational and administrative skills kick in to overdrive. First of all, I cancel the holiday I had booked to Sardinia for my 60th and after searching half a dozen sites of the cheapest fares to Malta, I returned to 'Dial a Flight', who I've used four times to various destinations and they always come up with the best flight routes/times at competitive prices. They do things properly and I highly recommend them. I didn't get tricked into buying a Ryan Air ticket for a bargain and then having the price bumped up because I actually want to take more than a pair of knickers with me on holiday!

The next thing was to decide to place myself strategically in terms of the geography of various places I wanted to be near. I want to explore both Malta and Gozo, so I've opted for the Luciano Valletta Boutique hotel, in Valletta for the first six nights. This will give me enough time to explore a great deal of this amazing historical small city. I'm then leaving for the quietness of rural Gozo and staying at the Ta'Kalmija B & B for six nights, based in the small village of Gharb, which looks delightful. I know I'm going to love Gozo and think it quite probable that it will be there, I choose to live. Yet, I still have the rest of Malta to see, so I will spend the last seven days exploring as much of it as I can.

I start making lists. I start making phone calls. I go on line and get 'Felicity', my fairly ancient Ford Focus, (with a dubious paint touch- up on the driver door, done by me), value checked. About four hundred quid, taking into consideration, both her exterior and amount she's run around! So not really worth spending £785 on shipping her to Malta.

Looking online at houses to rent in Malta, thankfully a great many of them are fully furnished. This has given me options. The idea is to find a house to rent whilst I'm there, to take possession of sometime in July. I can then spend six months really exploring the two islands, then register with Agents for an unfurnished long let in the areas I'd like to be in. I'm certain I'll know in 24 hours whether I want to live in Malta, but giving myself six to twelve months before moving all my belongings over is a good idea I think. I probably won't find the perfect house, in the perfect location in the short time I have to look whilst on holiday, so unless I do, not having my stuff with me initially will be more convenient and save money.

Research into storage companies and international removers has revealed a minefield of alternatives and prices. Storage facilities can be found just about anywhere in your town or relatively close by. Bear in mind though that many of them are little more than containers in a yard and your stuff will get damp inside from condensation! I got quotes from half a dozen by looking online and having a firm in Bath come out to see me. A 20 x 8 container is what I require for shipping, AFTER having sold an awful lot of my belongings. I'm not paying to store or ship two ancient armchairs that I keep covered with throws! I've always disliked the dining room table. I've already taken bootfulls of stuff to the Dorothy House Hospice Charity. I shall be doing car boot sales. I have a dozen mature shrubs in beautiful pots, which I sadly cannot take, numerous house plants, office furniture, too many books, on and on it goes and

I realise I have far too many things and it's time to part company with them. I contact an Auction House to see what they think and what their charges are and I open an account on Gum Tree and test the water with a dehumidifier (pardon the pun). Thirteen people have viewed it, but so far no one has called. I will need to place around sixty adverts for everything I need to sell!

The Maltese Expat Forums are a wealth of useful information. Some are better than others and some charge, but there are a fair few of them, so I've just been scrolling through and found some very handy tips on the application process for residency, as well as the medical side of things.

THE DIARY BEGINS

12th March, 2016

The decision to let go of huge amounts of my belongings and a substantial amount of furniture, together with the burning of endless diaries, going back thirty years has been very satisfying. My dining room, now devoid of its table, which brought me a hundred quid, has been turned into a shop, with the already packed and labelled up boxes of stuff I'm keeping, now acting as display stands for what I'm selling. I am fortunate to live just outside the boundary of a legendary weekly local, called The BVM (Blackmore Vale Magazine), avidly devoured throughout Dorset, parts of Wiltshire and edging into Somerset. A huge circulation and a third of the price of my local newspaper!

Looking carefully through all my stuff – just way too much, I'm beginning to wonder if I might have been a male Bower bird in a past life! I've never collected junk – it's all perfectly respectable stuff – I've just acquired too much of it over the last forty years. The advert I placed in the BVM for £11.65 heralded three calls, the first at 9:00 p.m. by an exceedingly dodgy sounding bloke who inquired as to whether I had any silver, gold, sovereigns, or jewellery I wanted to get rid of. I replied in a manner that gave him all the assurance he needed to know that I didn't – more rather car boot stuff and some office furniture, kind of thing which dispatched him off the end of the line with speedy perfection. The second and third calls resulted in two visits and a total of £114 in sales. Success – huge amounts I don't now have to lug to a car boot sale and the prices paid were fair. The people have all been lovely and wished me all the best. They seem to be rather astounded when they hear that I'm simply packing up and leaving for Malta, on my own, without ever having been there and without knowing a single person who lives there. They can see my excitement and leave heavy laden and rooting for me.

Had quotes ranging from £195 to £1200 for moving one cubic metre of my stuff by boat immediately. This area is obviously a bit of a minefield and will require additional exploration. I've been given some excellent advice by several of the very nice removal men who've been out to quote. Just in time, I was given two sheets of A4 paper with things on that Customs will not allow you to import. Shells, any kind of wicker, horse tack – all kinds of odd things that you could really be caught out over. I retrieved my very old Conch shells from packing box number twelve and thought it disconcerting that out of the six men quoting, I was only given this information by one of them. I was also told by several to make sure the quotes I got included for the handling through Customs and delivery to my house. So I need to find out exactly what is not covered and likely costs if Customs decide to open up a shipment of my belongings.

There has to be a detailed packing list specifically for me, so I can easily identify what's in the boxes – 'Granny's blue dish' etc. and then another detailed packing list for the inventory and Customs inspection. Customs have to be kept happy because they cost a lot of money per hour if they decide they want to unpack your things! My sister can look after my Conch collection. I'm now packing lots of boxes and about to start number fourteen. Discovered there's cheap bubble wrap which is crap bubble wrap, so don't scrimp on buying this – get the quality stuff! The only rooms in the house that don't look awful are the sitting room and my bedroom. All else is chaos. I feel in limbo, counting the hours until my departure.

Of course at this point in time in UK history, the Brexit referendum is having a huge impact on the Euro and I'm really not sure if it might put a spanner in the works for me if we come out of Europe, but I'm not waiting. Plan is going ahead full steam. I have bought my Euros for my holiday at €1.27, but realise it's feasible the pound and euro could be far more equal in the future if the people vote to Leave. Just typical, now that I require a constant stream of Euros. If there's a vote to leave it will be entirely my fault!

30th March, 2016

The scaling down of one's clutter really is a cathartic thing to do, as is burning diaries that were generally written in order to purge myself of negative emotion, hurt and pain, or to record in fairly graphic detail, things of a sexual nature that I presumed at the time I would one day enjoy reading! Not the case. I certainly don't want anyone else reading them. My filing cabinet has now become slimmer of the year, as old out-of-date policies, Mint statements and the like get heaved and incinerated if dated outside the current year!

My dearest brother, Ian, made a suggestion last time I saw him which made perfect sense, but has put me under a little pressure. Based on his suggestion, I am moving out of the house three days before I go on holiday and will stay with my sister Angela when I get back, until I fly out for good on 21st June – can't hang around until July I've decided. That flight now booked. I will save huge costs towards the storage and removal by saving all that rent, council tax, TV license and utilities. No point going on holiday for the three weeks I need to decide where to live, whilst leaving my own house empty of all but belongings that can be stored for a fraction of my rent! It never occurred to me and of course Angela said she'd be more than happy for me to stay.

I have pre-booked excess baggage for final departure, with Air Malta, at a total price of £140 for 84 kilos, which have to be weighed into one each of 32kgs and one 20kg bag or box. Shipping 1 cubic metre was going to cost around £1,200 which is a quarter of the total removal cost, so I can't take out any of my framed artwork. The £195 quote I got for sending out my work was likely by criminals, so I ignored it. I will just have to put up with the fact that fifty framed paintings and photographic works are going to be stored with everything else until I can ship all my belongings over together.

I tackled my studio walls and floor today with a pan scrubber, scraper and white spirit. I re-painted the back splash-wall the lovely chocolate plum it was before I turned it into a rudimentary Jackson Pollack, by frequently hitting the wall instead of my canvas with flying blobs of acrylic. Unfortunately I got the correct paint mixed up and I did a touch up coat with the left overs of my brothers more plum/lavender version of paint that in the tin looked very similar. On the wall, Jackson Pollack had transformed into Rothko!

Got stitched up by Sky who want £86 quid because I'm quitting my contract early. I specifically remember asking when I agreed to it that if I had to terminate because of emigrating, whether I would have to pay a termination fee and I was told no, only if I moved house in the UK and didn't take it with me, or moved to Virgin. Of course when I told the woman this, she 'checked the records' and there's no mention of this conversation in there! In my view Sky is in the same category as BT – they prostitute themselves to get your business and then fleece you when you become a customer. *Addendum 23ʳᵈ May on holiday; despite clearly telling Sky I was emigrating, they have hassled me continually with phone calls to my mobile, which at the moment, when abroad, costs me money whenever I receive a call or text. It got to a point where I had seen this particular number had been trying to contact me whilst on holiday about eight times. I didn't recognise the number but it was a normal UK landline, so I picked up call number nine and sure enough it was Sky trying to persuade me I'd made the biggest mistake of my life by leaving them! I'm afraid the caller got a very angry flea in his ear and I then blocked the number.*

1st April, 2016

Today is auction collection day. First load has gone and I'm watching the clock as payment is by the hour at a rate of £40 for a van and two men. The garden has been denuded of all my beloved plants and pots and an army of chairs cluttering the dining room has left a huge space. The overall effect is that it looks as though I now don't have a huge amount of stuff to store and ship – hopefully this will affect the perception of the last estimator coming out this afternoon to quote. Prices from various firms have differed by astonishing amounts – from £3,000 to £5,450, some inclusive of insurance, others not. Men and van now up to £60 and they're not back yet for load two. At least there's not much left to take, but adding in travel time and unloading at the Auction house, I reckon my bill for transport will be about £120.

10th April, 2016

Still not appointed Removal Company, but will do so this week by Wednesday. Starting to panic slightly and pray that it will all happen smoothly on the now immovable date of 4th of May and I find myself twiddling my thumbs because I need more boxes. The Auction was a big mistake. I was offered £40 for my filing cabinet on eBay and turned it down. It sold for £1.00 at the auction. I would not ever recommend putting anything in an auction unless you have an Old Master you want to flog. Buyers from eBay may not pay the price you're optimistically hoping for, but they will pay a realistic price, largely because they actually want what you're selling. In an auction, there will be things that people don't want, but will buy anyway because they can get it for a pittance and the interest of the Auctioneer in these kind of sales is to get through 900 lots by 4:00 p.m., so they are NOT working in your best interests. My office desk with a retail value of about £800 went for £3! A Tilley lamp I thought might get a couple of quid went for £28, which was a minor plus in the meagre calculations resulting in what others wished to pay for what I wanted to sell. The sales figures achieved with all my beautiful pots and plants nearly made me cry! eBay may have been much more work on my part, but it would have earned me far more.

12th April, 2016

Finally appointed Removal Company today after further delay of nine days for a quote from the last Company I rang. Very unprofessional and did not give me any sense of trust or reliability, so have gone for a highly accredited firm that are professional and will give me peace of mind, at a rate that has been the lower side of the prime remover quotes. I'm attached to my stuff, have a lot of paintings and work to store and want it well looked after and insured.

19th April, 2016

The countdown to removal day is down to fifteen days. I have loads of things still to do, though most of the packing is done. Telly has now gone, via eBay and I'll be glad to say goodbye to the addiction of television, but will HAVE to see the endings of 'Indian Summer', 'The Durrell's' and 'Undercover' or I'll go into decline! The biggest challenge at present is to organise the baggage to take out with me when I go for good.

As the date gets nearer for the EU vote, it feels like a countdown to my life in Malta beginning, as the two events are within two days of each other. I shall be living in Malta on the 21st June and have arranged for my sister to vote by Proxy for me. Like most people in the UK, I feel I don't have enough information to vote correctly, yet I know that for me, emigrating to Malta, my vote is naturally going to be to stay. If however I were remaining in the UK, I think I might vote to leave. I do absolutely believe we should never have joined in the first place – that was the error made by us as a country. This is simply my own opinion, or how I feel about it all, without yet having the actual facts and figures in front of me in an unbiased manner in order to make an informed decision. Will the population be armed with all the facts and information they need before they vote? It's certainly not looking promising as yet, all I've seen is political bickering.

My instinct is telling me and I'm usually right, that the vote will be to leave, but it will be very close. I would have voted NOT to join if we'd had a Referendum back then. Now? It's complicated. If it's Leave, what will happen to all those Brits who have emigrated to Spain, Portugal, France or Italy, who have homes and some have jobs or businesses? What about the poor Gibraltans? Sterling will drop like a stone, which is clearly not good news for me, turning it into Euros. I wonder what effects the Brexit decision will have on emigration to Malta, if any, other than currency issues. I don't think anyone really knows how the dominos will fall in terms of the timing or the cause and effect of Brexit, but financially it will be immediate and global.

So as removal day draws closer, whilst I can still burn a diffuser with Neal's Yard Frankincense, write with curtains drawn, candles flickering and a comfortable chair to sit on, I realise that I've got to get my arse in gear, sort out my baggage, pack more boxes and finish all my paperwork this week, so that I am absolutely ready for the removers. I have windows to clean and some sweeping to do. I need to go to the tip and to the charity shop, yet again. I still have the curtains and poles to take down in my bedroom and the sitting room, plus filling in all the nail holes and touching up the paint work. I panic that I'll never be ready and then can't seem to get anything done.

22nd April, 2016

A rather persistent spot that started as a blister on my upper chest, turned into more of a wart and finally into the makings of a small cruciferous vegetable, led me once again into the walk-in clinic in my town. Two doctors and the pharmacist at Boots had looked at this strange spot/growth weeks ago and dismissed it. The third doctor, a young GP looked at it and wanted to consult a more experienced colleague who immediately said I should be referred to a consultant Dermatologist. I decided then and there to use my private health insurance. A week after that appointment with my doctor, I had a squamous cell carcinoma removed. It was a big shock – I was imagining a cyst from an ingrown hair as I have occasionally

14

looked down at my breasts to discover a rather long, straight, protruding, single hair sprouting from my bosom in a rebellious abandonment of propriety. This however was no such triviality of manners, it was a result of too much radiation on my skin from the sun.

I have taken it entirely as the obvious warning shot across the bow that I needed, being a total beach bum and sun buff about to holiday and emigrate to Malta. Stay out of the sun Fiona! It will utterly cook my skin. It's not far from the African coast and much nearer to the equator than England and the sun is way too strong for me to be lying about in it getting a tan. In fact those days are now totally over. These squamous cells are a result of a build-up of long term UVB and UVA radiation, which of course I have had, growing up in Bermuda and going on holiday to the beach at every opportunity I've had. I blame my father, who was often caught out by the Vicar when visiting unannounced, totally 'starkas' on the back lawn, reading the paper and joining up his freckles. I have done exactly the same and love being outside as much as possible. I hate being indoors unless it's cold, so the sun and I are very well acquainted, clearly to the detriment of my poor skin which has been fried to within an inch of its life, and is now most determinedly telling me, "Skin is not meant to be cooked"!

Thank God for private health insurance. It would not have been good for this thing to have hung around. It was growing daily and was quite tender. I have to now watch all my skin with the tenacity of a Chimp scouting for lice and have it professionally checked once every six months for the next two years. Although I'm prone to getting these because of my fair skin, slightly red tint to my hair and previous relationship with the sun, I will not necessarily get another one. My input into making sure I don't is to no longer sunbathe and boost my immune system with a detox and ingestion of really nutritious chemical free, mostly vegetarian food and lots of exercise. I was planning on doing this anyway. A time for mediation and yoga, but now even more so. A time for reflection and connection to the inner me that is the higher self and connected to the Source of all creativity and consciousness. A time to see that this is the time to change and grow. To love those blessed genes I inherited from my father – the athletic physique, frame and ability to be flexible, fit and strong. Yes, I inherited his ginger gene and was a carrot haired toddler and the only one in the family as freckly as Daddy. I've not been enamoured of my fair Celtic skin and always rather envied the dusky olive complexion of the Mediterranean cultures. Their skin would never resemble an old Rhinoceros when viewed in a certain light! Time to start loving my skin methinks!

Thankfully I heal well and despite having a piece cut out of me that was about an inch across and three quarters of an inch deep. I looked at this chunk and concluded it was about the size of a Nouvelle cuisine appetiser. It required some stitching up and will leave me with abstract art on my décolleté and perhaps a slightly raised right breast. "Well, that's fine, just get rid of this alien cabbage thing that's got stuck on me and doesn't feel as though it's a part of my body at all". A week before my sixtieth birthday, I hardly think it's going to matter if the spirt level is a little out on the geometrics of my breasts and if f I ever do have sex again, hopefully neither he nor I will notice.

1st May, 2016

The two arm chairs I need gone by Tuesday didn't sell on eBay, even for free. It was the Independent market today, so I thought I'd ask the dealers if they wanted them. After all they are Edwardian chairs with original material, wooden ball feet and brass casters. Beautifully made chairs which I've had in my home for twenty years, worth diddly squat, but would be great recovered, which I never got around to doing. I hate waste and don't have the heart to tell the chair's that unless I find a rescuer, there will be no more bums on seats. Thankfully a furniture dealer called Shaun said he'd collect them, much to the chairs' and my relief. Fingers crossed he keeps his word.

3rd May, 2016 – last night before removal day

Chair Shaun turned up, as did a man for the telly who got a bargain of £50 for the 29" I advertised, but when I got out the original box from the cellar, it stated that it's in fact a 32"specimen. I could have kicked myself and wondered if he might offer something that might at least buy a small round at the pub, but he never did and I felt a bit like he'd robbed a granny. Just sooo glad to be rid of the chairs and the fridge, which went at 6:00 p.m. this evening. Wine now in the washing up bowl filled with cold water, communing with the milk for the removal men tomorrow. There's now rather less wine than there was a couple of hours ago and I'm a little within the bounds of my cups, but hey, I'm enjoying myself, though typing is tediously slow, amongst the bombardment of corrections. Miss Devlin, my formidable English teacher, pales into insignificance compared to the criticism of my mistakes by Microsoft Word!

EXPERIENCE OF THE ISLANDS ON HOLIDAY

10th May, 2016

Arrived in Malta to wet windy and decidedly chilly weather. Since I left the UK in its first mini heat wave, albeit one that was only due to last about three days, I couldn't help but see the irony of it, especially as my main reason for emigrating is the British weather. I was quite shocked to see from the air how built up the island actually is – far more so than I could have imagined and I <u>was</u> expecting it to be built up, but there are a few scattered bits of land amongst the buildings which seem to cover most of the island.

11th May, 2016

I took a horse drawn carriage ride around the perimeter of Valletta today, but got stitched up with the price, which to be fair, I should have bargained for. I'd do the same if I had a horse and cart business, but it was certainly not worth €50 and I realised afterwards that I had misheard him and that it was €15, so it was his lucky day! Then took a bus tour via the southern red route – a bus service where you can hop on and off wherever you like and I hoped off in Marsaxlokk, a once quaint fishing village, that's wonderful at dawn, but not at lunch time!

Valletta itself is lovely and very easy to walk around without getting lost, though it can be very up and down so good exercise. Found an M & S which had a very contemporary coffee bar and restaurant and was unlike any English M & S I've ever seen – perhaps a trial of some kind for them, but I don't think it would work in the UK. Looking forward to exploring the city by nightfall this evening as I was too knackered to do anything last night, but be in bed by 9:30 p.m. People are friendly and good looking and the Maltese women dress very well – no scruffy stuff here.

The food I have sampled so far has been very good and the wine is excellent, pure and very quaffable. Typically in the Med, if you order wine at a decent place, they often also bring you nibbles which can sometimes be a meal in itself if you don't have a big appetite. You can spend €4 on a large glass of wine that arrives with a bowl of dried broad beans, a bowl of fresh green olives and a bowl of crisps, at no cost, so have discovered that if I drink enough, I can eat for free, but clearly I won't remember anything about my holiday! It's things like this which make the term 'Rip off Britain' ring true, when I think about the smaller glass of wine in the pub I adored at home which costs £6.50 and nothing with it but a paper napkin! The temptation to drink too much is daunting though and when I've been told to stick to 14 units a week and to stay out of the sun because of my skin – I really should be looking at emigrating to Greenland and drinking nothing but Yak dung tea. I don't think so!

Gozo is what I need – a new Rock. The simple quiet life in a more rural idyll with fresh Gozitan grown vegetables and getting around on my bike and two legs and finding deserted beaches and rocky outcrops that no one but the locals know about, no traffic congestion, a green and environmentally sound island is what I'm craving really. So I'll walk and drink my way around Valletta for another five days and hope that Gozo provides me with a place I want to hang my hat and stay for a while, or emigrate to for the foreseeable future.

13th May, 2016

Took the blue bus tour today and saw another part of Malta and the more I saw, the less I thought I'd like to live there, although passing through Rabat and Mdina they looked quaint and interesting so will explore them further. Part of what I need creatively is visionary beauty through nature, architecture and scenery and unfortunately it looks as though Malta is somewhat lacking in this requirement. Although Valletta is lovely and met my expectations, generally Malta is not a pretty island architecturally because so many of the character houses and older properties have been torn down or bombed in the war. There's also a distinct lack of trees. It looks far better at night, when you can't see all the bare rocky ground, separated by armies of dry stone walls and cranes spoiling the sky line in all urban areas, continually being developed or re-built. Passing through St Julien's and Sliema, I could only thank God that I didn't make plans to stay there. I admit though that so far, I have only seen the major tourist routes and will reserve my final judgement when I come back here on the 19th for my final week and am able to explore by car on my own.

Am slightly in panic mode – what if I really don't like Gozo either? With the Referendum looming large on 23rd June, I can't simply decide to emigrate to Italy, which I know I adore, but I haven't a clue about all the things I looked into regarding Malta and why it would be such a great place to live outside the UK. I can't suddenly switch to Italy or Sicily. What about the health service? Could I trade in island life for mainland Italy, France or Spain? Right now a shack on a beach in the Caribbean feels more 'me' than anywhere on this busy traffic mad island. I had a feeling right from the start regarding Malta that it would be Gozo I'd prefer, so hoping with very crossed fingers that I will love it.

Had an interesting evening and experienced my first prejudice against a lone diner tonight. There was a male lone diner too but he had arrived earlier than me so no chance of a merger and I wondered if he felt equally insignificant. I had wanted more parmesan on my risotto (which by the way and quite truthfully, was not as good as my own) yet once my meal was served I was ignored, as if some rather embarrassing part of the furniture. I read my book, as I always take my Kindle when out and about with no-one to talk to when I'm eating or drinking on my own. It stops you having to pretend to study the décor with huge interest because you have nothing else to do when there's nobody to talk to. I'm reading a rather a good book by Edward Rutherford, called 'The Forest' all about the New Forest from about 1099 to 1400AD. I ate, paid and slipped out like a silent being who had never even been there. I certainly wasn't hanging around for goodbyes and platitudes of the wonderful chef. I could beat him hands down with a risotto fungi. The waiter had done the minimum possible in order to serve me any food at all and didn't deserve anything for his meagre efforts. Will certainly not be going there again. Surely a good restaurant should look after a woman on her own with even more care than a mixed table of four – I guess not in their case. Perhaps I should have ordered four bottles of wine! C'est la vie!

19th May, 2016

I arrived in Gozo three days ago and thankfully I love it! It's a completely different kind of island to Malta with more greenery, space and quiet roads, lots of hills and wonderful views and a much slower pace of life with far less traffic and fresh sea air. One can only hope the Maltese Government maintain the quiet rural charm of Gozo. It's most certainly already changed considerably from when Google Earth last updated their satellite imagery! Not a crane in sight here right now thankfully and the only traffic to contend with is in Victoria and it pales into insignificance compared to most of Malta.

Picked up my hire car which I have named Mudwort, due to its metallic brown colour. The power steering is amazing and especially necessary driving in Gozo, but it has less torque than a tortoise, so spend much time in second gear. The hills are sometimes steep, the roads often filled with potholes and drain covers that sit up out of the road like sentinels daring you to drive over them. Tyres in Gozo live in a constant state of fear and persecution. I haven't seen many expensive cars here and I have to say, having one would be very restrictive in terms of the roads you would find acceptable to drive down in a car worth more than €5000! If the bumpy roads or drain covers don't ruin it, the dust most certainly will. I don't want to give the wrong impression here – there are some good roads to the main places, but there are so many other 'off piste' places waiting to be explored. Roads that exist, but as little more than partly concreted tracks, full of potholes, beckoning you to drive over cliffs that lead to secret beaches, or down into mystical valleys of abundant vibrant green, speckled with tanned farmers carefully tending their crops.

20th May, 2016

You can drive from one end of Gozo to the other in about twenty minutes and I have explored most of island in two days with the voracity of a hornet with hemorrhoids, in order to find which town I would like to live in. Victoria, the capital, is too busy and the pretty back lanes are somewhat closed-in, so I've been to all the other villages, seen every beach, sussed out all I needed to know and decided on the village I want to be in. I chose Xaghra, so then marched off to the Estate Agents to view available flats. They are like hens teeth at this time of year and are quickly snapped up. I viewed two, the first being what I had imagined, one step up from camping and a pittance of a rent compared to the UK, but I really didn't think I'd be either comfortable or happy living there for a month, let alone six. I saw another, more expensive, but still a shed load cheaper than my UK rent and immediately knew I would like living there. It's a new build, modern, well furnished, though slightly Maltese in terms of taste, which tends to be rather ornate with huge chandeliers and a bit too much bling for my liking, but very comfortable beds, a decent well equipped kitchen, air con and heating, plenty of space and a small balcony with a view to die for. I said I would take it. That settles it then – I'm emigrating to Gozo for at least six months!

23rd May, 2016 – back in Malta

I spotted the Paradise Bay Hotel (overlooking the Ferry Terminal) into which I've booked the last week of my holiday in Malta, when I got the ferry to Gozo. "Oh hell" I thought as I surveyed the painted concrete façade, "I don't think I'm going to enjoy it there"! Sure enough, arrival today confirmed my worst fears. I was initially shown to a room that wasn't large enough to swing a cat in and made me feel very claustrophobic just being in there momentarily. I politely stated that it would not do and could I have a larger room please. I had requested on the Booking.com site, a double bed as I find single beds very unhomelike when compared to my Queen sized Vi-Spring. A double bed could not be found, but I did get a bigger room that wasn't the equivalent of a Drury Lane dressing room, which the previous one most certainly had been. I'm very much a person to rate my stays with Booking.com and after this, I'm not sure I will actually use them again. They are good for finding deals and I cannot fault the B & B in Gozo I left this morning, but the hotel in Valletta wasn't quite what I had expected and most certainly this one is not up to scratch by my standards at all.

Spent the afternoon traipsing the second hand car dealers in Quormi (Malta capital for car dealers) and discovered that unless you are happy to pay about €6000 for a car, what you get offered can be pretty naff, with high mileage and no service records. To get an equivalent car to my Ford Focus that had 106,000 miles on the clock and was worth £450 in the UK, it will cost me about €1,700 here. Importing cars from the UK however is expensive not only in shipping, but the tax you then have to pay. The tax payable varies on the model of car and year of manufacture, but it can be steep, so look into this carefully. At the time of writing, you can import your car without having to pay tax if you have owned it for two years prior to importation. If you do decide it's worth importing, you need to very quickly get your license plate changed to a Maltese one, in about a month I believe, otherwise you'll be charged even more. The higher the value of your car and the newer the model, the more tax you'll have to pay, but it may still be cheaper to import your car if you have one that is worth more than 8K. Those costs are certainly not worth paying for a run-around motor, but if you have a decent car, the shipping and tax you may have to pay would still be cheaper than buying a posh car here.

Tomorrow I plan to investigate Paradise Bay beach, on which the hotel does NOT sit and without a car it's a 15 minute walk uphill. The guide books say that there are some interesting things to see in this quiet rural area, so I'm certainly up for the challenge to prove them right or wrong. There may be some interesting photography at the Popeye village and there are some incredibly ancient ruins around here somewhere and good walks to be had. To be honest though, I now just want to get back to the UK so I can then get back to Gozo and start my new life and I have to say sitting here, I miss that island a little bit already.

The Gozitans are so friendly, happy and chilled out. Although most of the Maltese are friendly too, it's a very different way of life on the big island and the stress and bustle of the place naturally rubs off on some of the people who are a tiny bit angst ridden and stressed. Truthfully, at this stage I'm a little frightened by my commitment to stay in Gozo for six months. I worry slightly that it's just too small and too quiet and even at the ripe old age of 60, I still like to party, listen to bands and dance and at the very least have the choice of joining in with the big wide world. I'm concerned that in Gozo maybe what you're essentially signing up for is signing out and I fear it may be too quaint and too quiet for me to live there long term, but six months should be fine.

25th May, 2016

Have car will travel, especially as the Paradise Bay hotel is even worse than I first thought. Yesterday morning I left at 7:15 a.m. with a determination to be the first to arrive at the Ghar Dalam caves just out of Birzebbugia. They were difficult to find as the signage in Malta is rather sporadic, but I arrived just before 9:00 a.m. and had the caves and museum entirely to myself. The cave is impressive and the collection of bones in the museum incredible because of their sheer number. Just as I was leaving the car park at 9:45 a.m. the first coach load arrived, so I was rather chuffed with myself. I then drove on through the more rural area of Malta, west of Birzebbugia towards Zurrieq and on to the Hagar Qim and Mnajdra Temples – apparently one of the most ancient structures in the World. Thoroughly fascinating, as was the 3-D film they show, where you have to don special specs. I have never experienced 3-D before and I loved it! I could quite happily have sat and watched it a dozen times, but unfortunately there are breaks between showings, so I just got on and visited the two temples. They are both protected with giant white UVB/UVA filter domes which are very necessary as the elements are degrading the stone and these afford some protection, though the Government are still looking into what can be done to preserve them less intrusively.

The driving around in this area if you're willing to go 'off piste' and take a chance down the bumpy roads is well worth the journey – the views are incredible and the area very rural, as is the far east of the island, beyond Rabat to the coast. Hiring a car and sightseeing is the only way to really explore somewhere. What you see and get on the tour guide bus routes is not by a long way, all there is. Whilst the rural areas were a vast improvement on the hustle and bustle of the busy areas, they are so remote as to offer nothing unless you get in your car and travel to the bustle, which for me would be far too much of a pain, but they would be ideal for those who really want to shut away the world in peace and quiet.

The area around Buskett was beautiful with an ancient Chateau and the most flora, fauna and trees I've seen on the whole island. My wish for Malta would be the planting of lots more trees and shrubs everywhere, but perhaps the climate is too dry and plants have to be watered regularly - I'm not sure at this stage. The island was once covered in trees and eons ago was linked to Sicily by land bridges, which is why there are Elephant and Hippo bones here that were found in the cave. During the last Ice Age, mammals came to Malta to find a more temperate climate.

Spent a lazy day today on the large sandy beach at Melliah Bay. The beach resembles an army from Game of Thrones in sheer number of umbrellas and sunbeds and by 11:00 a.m. most of them are occupied. It was my first day spent on the beach since my holiday began over two weeks ago and I had forgotten how wonderful it is, even when staying in the shade of the umbrella. A good book of course is de-rigour, but people watching has always been a favourite pastime too. The shapes, sizes, colour's and variety of people was quite magnificent. Fat ones, thin ones, red ones, tattooed ones, black ones, brown ones, very white ones, young, old and everything in between speaking a variety of languages. Of course, as any woman who's honest will admit to, you do compare your own figure with those on display. Carrying 'a little holiday weight right now', I feel my stomach is not its svelte self and kept my shirt on, as much for sun exposure as vanity, but in fact felt rather pleased that my figure is not too bad for a Granny who's now a Senior citizen in Malta! Most of the bods on the beach were very ordinary, but happily there were two gorgeous bodies equal to the physique of David Gandy and hiding behind my dark sunglasses, I just sat there secretly staring away imagining being rescued by either or both of them from a pre-historic Rhino or something. They certainly distracted me from my book!

The beach is ideal as the water is shallow and protected from most of the wind, so it's great for children. There are kiosks selling water, ice cream and British newspapers and a number of restaurants along the quay, several of which looked rather good. I wandered off down the quay to a watering hole and sat and had a glass of wine and people watched. It was quite extraordinary and highly amusing.

I've never really understood the obsession for selfies and on the odd occasion the camera on my phone has accidently reversed itself and I've clapped eyes on myself, the image is enough to frighten small children and make me want to wear a bag on my head for the rest of my life. I sat secretly watching a couple in their twenties and the woman was obviously a professional selfie taker and proceeded, rather to the embarrassment of him, to whip out a long white stick and wave it four feet in the air and then sit posing, attempting a number of different 'looks' whilst clicking away. Said stick was then lowered, the phone unclipped, images examined and then the whole process started again. He was quietly trying to read a guide book on Malta and very aware that people were watching this procedure with wry amusement and he wasn't very happy about it and couldn't have cared less about the results from the waving stick.

Another couple walked in, younger, wearing little, tattooed and pierced and she had jet black hair coiled up into a bun on the back of her head, but both sides of her scalp had been shaved. Her arms were entirely covered in designs and I have to wonder at people's tastes – thank goodness we're all different and it's good practice not to be judgemental simply because tastes in attractiveness are so vehemently opposed to your own!

Perhaps the funniest couple however were the typically British mid 40's pair who had been sitting for a while waiting to be served. In Malta, service is not quick – nearly always pleasant, but never in a hurry and you can easily find yourself waiting ten to fifteen minutes to even be noticed in a great many establishments. He was reading 'Funny Girl', she something I couldn't see, but they were obviously hungry and the wife had clearly told him to "do something" about attracting attention. He put his book down and started waving at bustling waiters, all to no avail! His wife looked at him with disdain at his pathetic attempt to attract the attention of anyone other than me and his ineptitude at politely trying to request service. I could tell he felt like a complete prawn and he rather sheepishly went back to his book for a few minutes before trying the same thing all over again, still to no avail! By this time, I had almost finished my glass of wine and when the waitress came to the table next to mine to deliver food, just as she was turning away, I asked in a loud enough voice for her to hear me "could I have my bill please". She turned and acknowledged my request, but the poor unfortunate man had had his back to her, so missed the opportunity to catch her attention. His wife then gave him a look of pure venom that clearly thought "for goodness sake, even a Granny on her own is better at getting service than you are"! Poor man – I think they might still be waiting for their lunch. I returned to the beach with a smile on my face, thankful for the great side show to my glass of tincture.

26th May, 2016

Inquired this morning at the 'Entertainment desk' of the disappointing hotel I'm staying in, about boat trips and was told I'd have to drive to Sliema. Horror of horrors – attempt all that traffic and fumes in the heat of a Monday morning which would take ages and ditto the drive back. "Really", I exclaimed, "I'm not driving all the way to Sliema – don't you know of anywhere closer"? She told me that their Company did not depart from anywhere else and she was conveniently not aware of anything closer. I drove down to Mellieha and found a boat large enough to supply food, drinks and a loo and for €13, that would pootle about drifting over to Comino, the caves, stopping for snorkeling and I could enjoy the ride from 11:00 a.m. until 4:00 p.m. I got on and had a delightful day on the 'English Rose'. How interesting that the hotel tourist guide didn't know about a boat tour right on their doorstep!

Got showered, changed and put on a face with the idea of eating at the Paradise Bay Beach restaurant, a short drive away, which has a very good, though typically rather moody Chef. Sadly, I realised, before descending the huge number of steps down, that it looked rather deserted. I did that very typical British thing and asked some foreigners, (who were speaking a language totally unrecognisable to me), in the same manner I would talk to the Vicar, whether the restaurant was open. Despite me not understanding their language, I understood enough of the reply to know that one of the group exclaimed in his own tongue, words to the effect of my audacity at expecting them to understand me! Realising my assumption of their ability to speak English had insulted him, I then sheepishly asked if they "spekenze Englaise" and one replied she did a little and managed to tell me the restaurant was only open for lunch.

What is it about the Brits? If they're not deep into their cups, totally unintelligible and somewhat letting the side down, they assume everyone speaks their language? Perhaps some reminiscent thing in our genes concerning the Empire? Guilty as charged, certainly on the latter – actually, probably both. Disappointed and not wanting to drive very far at all, as I fancied having a glass of wine or two, I decided to go back to a hotel restaurant I went to several nights ago, just down the road, which appeared to be a public restaurant. It had been quite a good menu but I chose rather badly at the time and did not enjoy curried risotto. I thought to give it another chance and that anything would be an improvement on what's on offer at the 'Hell Hole' hotel in which I'm unfortunately staying (my own opinion of course).

I took a seat at a vacant table, but after five minutes or so, realised there appeared to be no waiting staff at all. I got up and ambled over to the Chinese place next door, but didn't fancy the menu, so sloped back to the cocktail lounge next to the restaurant I had previously eaten in and ordered a glass of wine. This is where it got interesting. Not looking my best by a very long way, due to the copious amounts of wine and pasta I've consumed whilst being on holiday, I'm puffy, with bags under my eyes, no cheek bones in evidence at all and if my phone camera decided right now to reverse itself, I'd probably want to die. Nevertheless, a rather attractive waitress at the cocktail bar clearly fancied me no end. It's the first time in my life I've ever been so clearly mesmerizing to a member of my own sex. It was not unwelcome – dear God at this stage of such A-sexual non activity in my life, I'd be glad to be fancied by a cabbage, but by an attractive woman, I couldn't help but smile and be inwardly chuffed that I'd scored!

It transpired that this bar was for hotel users only, the kind who wear wristbands and get booze for free, but she told me she could sell me a half bottle of a very nice Maltese wine for €7. I agreed and she fussed around me after I'd sat down and told me there would be live music starting in about half an hour and I could happily vape away indoors with no problem. On inquiring about food, she offered to make me a plate of cheese and salami, but I told her I didn't eat that kind of meat, quite innocently and truthfully and declined the platter. However, I just know that after some reflection, she was wondering just what kind of meat I did eat! I didn't have the heart to say that I did like the odd sausage, but only the ones that were kind of stuck on to people like Daniel Craig or Aiden Turner, otherwise it was pretty much just chicken!

I read my book for a while and then started to get a bit peckish. The trouble was that the public restaurant I had dined in a few nights ago had turned into a pick and mix buffet for guests of the hotel. Everyone was wearing wrist bands and belonged there, free to pick and choose from mountains of food, all pre-paid with their package. It was a feeding frenzy conveyor belt for hotel guests and clearly the public restaurant of the other night had disappeared. Disappointed, but hungry enough to eat a bear, I committed a sin! Pouring out the rest of the bottle, my glass full, I walked into the restaurant, found a table, put my glass down on it and trying desperately not to attract attention, purposefully walked over to the buffet. I hastily pulled down the sleeves of my jumper! I was waiting for the men in black to tap me on the shoulder and tell me I didn't belong, but with the panache of someone who did and being a woman on her own of a certain age, I helped myself to the buffet. Granted, I only had a small bowl of pasta and cous cous with a few green leaves for decoration and iron, though it wasn't really enough to feed a fairy, I munched my way through it quickly and guiltily and got up and left. I was ashamed that I felt rather pleased with myself and entertained fantasies of eating like a King for the next two nights of my holiday buckshee, but to be honest, I really don't have that kind of nerve. I worry about Karma. I had gone there with the intent of sitting down and paying for a meal, but that clearly wasn't an option, so I just took paupers portions to prevent starvation. Clearly this evening was some kind of test for my soul regarding sex and food, which I certainly failed, being moderately chuffed with both scenarios that are normally quite out of my hemisphere, not being either a thief or a lesbian. I'm still giggling about both and still rather pleased with myself.

27th May, 2016

I've become like a dog with a bone concerning the terribly disappointing hotel I'm staying in and have done a very severe letter of complaint to Booking.com and taken photos to prove my allegations. The list is long, but the air conditioner is worth mentioning. Naturally it should switch off if you leave your balcony sliding door open. Not good for the environment trying to air condition the outside World, but the tenacity of this air conditioner means that if you want your room cooled down before bed and want to sit out on your balcony writing this, if you open the sliding door half an inch the thing shuts off, yet doesn't come on again when you close the door, IF you remain outside. If you come back in and close the door, it comes back on. How on earth does this air conditioner know whether I'm in the room or on my balcony? How does this work? How does an air conditioner know whether I'm outside or inside my room? It has me mystified and searching for covert cameras. It's simply disgraceful and typical of these money grabbing owners of a hotel, clearly out to make money and screw over their guests. If they'd bothered to fit screens, I wouldn't even need the air conditioning, but I don't fancy getting got by mozzies again after one bit me on my face and swelled up my right eye for two days, which was, I hasten to add, prior to the sinning. The thermostat is also hotel set at a mediocre temperature, so you can't have it cold enough to be comfortable all night without it feeling stuffy. Considering AC's not even needed at this time of year, surely if they want to save money fitting screens would be cheaper.

I have made a pact with myself never to stay in another crappy hotel in my life. I swear I'd rather camp than do this and save myself shedloads of dosh for something that is so frustrating rather than any kind of comfort. I took photos of the outlook from the hotel beach today – a wonderful view of the Ferry Terminal and a wind turbine. They don't put that on the brochure do they? Rant over – sorry! Two more days of hell hole and then back to UK until 21st of June and then to my new home in Xaghra, Gozo.

4th June, 2016

Have been back in the UK since the 28th of May and staying at my sister's in Somerset. The green of England was wonderful to come back to and there will never be anything to compete with the English countryside on a summer day in May or June.

I accept that and relish it while I can. The great summer days are like diamonds dropped from God on this ancient green land and I could never fail to be moved by them. Yet I know they are a scarcity, with far more grey and cold than is acceptable to me in the longer term. I wait with each passing day for my return home to Gozo and the start of my new life in the Mediterranean – the fresh food, loads of Gazpacho, Gozitan sheep's cheese, the cool dawn mornings with breezy evenings and days so hot one can only sleep from noon to four in the afternoon, or write or paint whilst remaining indoors, especially for me.

I've discovered much about sun tan lotion and the conclusion so far is that the best, less chemical kind, is the sort that will make me look rather like dear Tudor Queen Bess. A white patina or sheen of gloop that is protection without the awful chemicals, pure zinc oxide which looks no more fetching on me than it did on Elizabeth Ist. Every time I wear it, I want to state "I am married to England Lord Burghley". I'm becoming a bit obsessed with sun screen and am determined to find some that's not made with plutonium equivalents, but that doesn't make me look as though I'm about to audition for the latest 'Corpse Bride' instalment. I'm slightly pissed off with my mother for allowing me to burn as a child, but equally pissed off with the misconception everyone has today that if you don't allow yourself to burn, you will be ok, because that's simply a lie. The sun on your skin for fifteen minutes a day is enough for vitamin D, but after that you are taking a big risk, especially so when you're not olive or brown skinned and don't have brown eyes. My search for the perfect sun screen continues.

11th June, 2016

As usual the British summer has been driving me nuts, with grey cold rain and wind and I'm frustrated with boredom and almost counting the hours until the 21st. Somerset has always been one of my favourite Counties and exploring the areas around Ham Hill and the surrounding exquisite countryside has been a welcome diversion. I've seen sleepy villages and been for some great walks amongst the rolling hills and valleys, listening to the calls of the buzzards circling high up on thermals as the sheep gently bleat to each other between mouthfuls of grass. This is the England I love best, but it helps so much when the sky is blue and the sun is shining and sadly this just doesn't happen enough for me. I don't like being cold.

My sister, Angela, is a peach especially for putting up with me and my huge amount of baggage for five weeks. Her sitting room floor is reduced in size by a large and very heavy tote bag and a big cardboard box and because she has little cupboard space in her kitchen, the counters are decorated by my foodstuff and far too many boxes of different types of tea. She's been very patient, but I have nearly gone demented with the weather and boredom, as there's no broadband, sky or virgin and a very minimal selection of dvd's, so I've nearly gone cross eyed reading so much. The overall effect on me has been some kind of taupe, so that I seem to have lost all motivation to do anything and I just want to be gone. No reflection on my dear sister, just that five weeks is a long time to wait to be somewhere else.

ARRIVAL IN GOZO, MALTA TO LIVE

21st June, 2016

The slight worry was always my baggage – excess without a doubt, booked before my flight, but I discovered at the airport that my scales have been lying to me and horror of horrors this does not just concern my luggage which told me it was 32 kilos when in fact it was nearer 34. I have obviously been deluded about my own weight too, that lying sod of a scale! 'Elf and Safety' will not allow anyone to lift more than 32 kilos so at check-in I had to divert to repacking and transfer excess 34 kilo weight into 20 kilo suitcase. Kindly, Air Malta did not then charge me extra for my 20 kilo case that became stuffed to the brim with another 2.8 kilos of weight! My taxi driver, Ramazan from Romania, was a sweetheart and took possession of one trolley, after parking the car and came right up to the check-in desk with me. On the journey he had plugged me into his phone and videos of Romania, whilst informing me that HRH Prince Charles and Camilla spend three months in Romania every year. I told him this was information us Brits were not privy to know, but after viewing the videos, I quite understand why. Romania is utterly stunningly beautiful.

After the re-pack, I dispatched bags to their relevant postings and all arrived on time and with me three hours later in Malta. I didn't cry when I left the UK but I cried with joy flying over Gozo and landing in Malta. A porter cost me €12 which I booked at the reception desk of the VIP enclave. A single youth who looked as though he might be part of a boy band, or perhaps just had very rich parents, was ensconced amongst the plush sofas and free gratuities, looking rather bored and impatient. My duly hired Porter arrived and was, to my mind, a saint as he waited patiently, beyond his clock off time whilst my very inadequate (as it turns out) car hire Company kept me waiting for the car. Once the keys were given to me, he pushed the heaviest trolley to the relevant hire pick-up point and put all the luggage in the car. The concerns of my sister who was clucking like a hen over how on earth I would manage all this baggage, together with my own slight reservations, turned out to be unjustified. If you have money to pay for something there is no problem and to be fair I had nowhere near as much luggage as Dame Joan would have on a quick weekend break!

Marlene, my landlady had it sorted when I got to my flat, by roping in her brother, Frank and his friend to lug it all up four flights of stairs, by which time poor Frank was about to expire from perspiration. They welcomed me to my new home with a vase of fresh flowers, a bottle of wine and half a dozen small bottles of water. How extraordinarily sweet and how totally Gozitan.

At 9:00 p.m. I decided to wander up to the Square to get a meal. There are actually five restaurants on Xaghra Square to choose from and I had an excellent tagliatelle with tomatoes, buffalo mozzarella and artichoke which was very tasty. I came back home, had a shower, opened the wine bottle and sat out on my balcony listening to the cicadas chirping away and peaceful quiet, other than them and the odd rustle of some animal in the garden below, a distant dog bark and the odd car passing. I feel like the luckiest woman alive. It's as though I've escaped a prison of grey, cold, damp/wet, busy noise, just in the nick of time. What was it Emma Thompson said to describe Britain? Something like a grey sodden Island filled with miserable people and a lot of cake? I quite agree. Don't get me wrong, anywhere in the British Isles on a beautiful Summer Day is one of the best places in the World to be, it's just that they happen far too infrequently for me to want to go on living there.

I sit here now listening to nothing but cicadas and my clicks on the keyboard. The temperature is a wonderfully warm, yet comfortably cool night and I know that in the South West of England, which I left this morning, sitting outside would be perishing even in mid-June. I so hated that about England. Have had the odd mozzie munch on my legs and feet though, so will have to cover up when sitting outside. You do end up being mozzie fodder in hot countries if you sit outside without protection. I'm so excited it's difficult to go to bed to sleep but it's now 12:30 a.m. Malta time, 11:30 p.m. in the UK and I am tired, so I think probably best to get into my new bed and try it out.

25th June, 2016

Discovered that the Maltese and Gozitans are extremely fond of fireworks, so much so that they let them off during the day with very little reason it appears. The appeal seems to be about the noise and the puffs of smoke appearing in the air against the azure blue sky. Last night there was an evening show, lasting far longer than any display in the UK and ending with bangs as loud as cannons firing at invaders. I will have a magnificent view on the 5th of November, assuming with the Maltese connection to Britain, that they celebrate Guy Fawkes here!

Got up at 5:00 a.m. this morning and was out walking just before 6:00 a.m. – a walk of about two miles which ended just as the great coffee café was opening at 7:00 a.m. as I reached the square in Xaghra. It was delightful being up before the sun was properly up and so it was of course cooler, though there was no breeze. A couple who were at least in their late 60's passed me on a moped. I thought they were very brave considering most of the road surfaces in Gozo.

Having been here for five days my priority now is to open a Maltese bank account which hopefully I shall be able to do and once it's open, I will be able to transfer from the UK via a Currency Exchange Company, rather than paying the exorbitant fees to withdraw small amounts at dreadful exchange rates, with high bank charges through my UK bank cards, which also place a fairly low limit per transaction. Thankfully I got a stash of Euros out, with a half reasonable rate before Brexit. Once I have a bank account opened, I am going to apply for Residency here as soon as possible.

It turns out opening a bank account here is not very easy! I initially went to the Bank of Valletta (BOV) but they were pedantic and not very customer friendly. Taking a good written reference into the bank from your UK Bank is not acceptable. I had to actually call my UK Bank and speak directly to the customer complaints department and explain that the BOV required a letter written by them to an actual person in Victoria, Gozo and then put into the snail mail post! This news was met with some incredulity by the exceptionally nice lady I was talking to. Highly irregular in terms of International Banking, but Santander UK came up trumps. Finally, the requested reference from my UK bank arrived at my Gozo bank and I now have an account. UK banks are rarely asked for references these days and tend to ignore Swift messages from foreign banks requesting one. Mine certainly did. The whole saga dragged on for nearly eight weeks. Banks do not communicate by email – at least this is a Bank of Valletta rule, so one to bear in mind if you plan to open an account here with them. I suppose it might be different if you had half a million to deposit, but sadly I didn't. I can't however have a bank card to pay for anything until I get a Maltese mobile because of the bank wanting to text me, every time I use my card and they won't text my UK mobile. Bit of a pain, but I can go in and withdraw cash, so I'll put up with it for now. There are other banks here, and after some years I would recommend BNF, rather than BOV for various reasons I won't go into here, but check them out before you decide to bank BOV.

I've discovered a few Galleries and there's a Maltese Art Society which I will join. There are events and things to do and there's a music scene and all I could wish for really. What is there not to love? How could this possibly not be better than anywhere in the UK, considering the weather difference?

Am slightly bothered by one thing though. I will admit to being a complete map Geek, inherited from my dear late father. I adore Ordnance Survey maps and especially love the orange ones that have even more detail on them. The maps here that I have found so far are devoid of the kind of detail I like to scrutinise. They don't even have all the names of places on, let alone all the roads. They are a complete farce for map aficionados and this is very disappointing to me. I like touring, map on seat and figuring out exactly where I am and where I want to go to. This is nigh on impossible anywhere in Malta or Gozo. It's more like a game of just drive and see what happens and where you end up. Consequently, if you don't have a sat nav, you never have the slightest clue where you are, or are able to find the road you want in order to get to your destination. Signage in Malta and Gozo is also frustratingly lacking. This is infuriating and clearly Malta needs some ace surveyors to map the country properly because even the airport isn't sufficiently signposted.

26th June, 2016

Good gracious it's 8:00 a.m. and I think I've heard some fireworks already! Yes, definitely fireworks. Perhaps they're used to get teenagers out of bed! No, I've just twigged it's nothing to do with teenagers, apparently it's Festa Season. Fireworks have been going off during the day, as clearly the bangs and puffs of smoke are greatly appreciated, but at night they really go to town. Hours and hours of fireworks. The noise is extreme and reverberates down through and across the valleys and hills and you hear echoes of the noise. It sounds rather like a film set for a war movie, but clearly this is what Festa season is like. I don't mind because I'm also a bit of a firework Geek too and love to photograph them. Today on my 'touring travels' I actually came across one of the firework factories, down another long bumpy unsigned road that I thought I'd just drive down. There were signs of danger! Clearly Malta and Gozo are not short of dynamite, but I suppose that would be the case when their history has had so many invaders. They have so much dynamite on these two islands that they can put on firework shows for five hours at a time in each small town and if it was all clubbed together, they could very clearly blow up the World. Does NATO know about this? Thankfully all bangs cease at about midnight, but don't plan on having a lie in. Perhaps things will return to normal as tomorrow is Monday.

As with all hot countries, in the summer life starts very early in the morning, then shuts down at 12:30 p.m. and opens once more from 4:00 p.m. to 7:00 p.m. Life picks up again in the evening, with most people out eating their supper between 8:00 and 10:00 p.m. One can't imagine doing that in the UK, but it's actually rather nice. Clearly until I get into the swing of things I shall be severely sleep deprived. Having woken up at dawn this morning, I'm still writing after midnight, but I don't actually feel tired, although I did try to have a Siesta this afternoon. I'm not used to a daytime zizz, but it's something I shall obviously have to get used to or I will look like Godzilla's Granny from lack of sleep. It's all just so exciting right now, I can't be bothered to sleep, especially if I have wine, which is inexpensive, not full of chemicals and tastes great.

Yesterday morning I went off to the beach early, simply because I could. A ten minute drive to San Blass Bay which sits at the bottom of the steepest hill I've ever walked up and it's a long hill, absolutely a killer walking back up it, so avoid that beach unless you're fit, or want to admit that you're not, in which case you can hire a Jeep to transport you up to the top for a couple of Euros (coward). I walk up because it's the greatest fitness training you can get, but it is NOT enjoyable.

Today I went off exploring by car again to some areas I've not yet seen, finding unpaved roads that look slightly scary, which draw me like a moth to a flame and I might end up in a quarry or somewhere I'll be told off, but show me a road less travelled and I'll want to drive down it. This curiosity is another thing I have inherited from my Daddy who used to do exactly the same thing on our childhood holidays in France and Spain and invariably we'd end up in a farmyard!

It's after midnight again and I'm writing this on my balcony and the night breeze has got up and it's actually quite chilly now – a blessed relief from the heat of the day. I don't as yet know how hot the nights will be in July, August and September, but certainly I appreciate the cooling down at night that June has provided – whether it's normal or not, I don't know. Another flurry of loud coloured dynamite has just gone off somewhere in the distance of this weekend's Festa town and it was most certainly the Grand Finale (one can only hope). A dog is barking, but I think Maltese pets are well used to fireworks and take them as the norm at certain times of the year, much like the variables in the weather.

At this hour, the restaurants have disgorged their satiated and hopefully happy customers and the non Festa participating Gozitans have abandoned their street chairs and positions of cool contemplation and retreated indoors. Another night time in Gozo where all becomes quiet and peaceful, apart from the wind, cicada chirping and the odd distant church bells ringing, unless the dogs start barking, which can be very irritating. The wind here can actually be quite vicious and sometimes is filled with sand from North Africa, or dust from the parched land that has seen little rain for months on end. I'm not looking forward to those times, as the best thing is to shut all the windows and doors unless you enjoy a massive clean-up operation of dust and dirt from here or Libya throughout your house. That will be the time to use the air conditioning! Yet even with the prospect of that, the only thing so far bothering me is the lack of a proper blasted map! And on that note, I really have to end my first weekend in my new home, in my new country and bugger off to bed!

2nd July, 2016 – second Saturday night

I don't know what it is about the weekend, whether you're self-employed or retired, there's still something about Friday and Saturday nights that the brainwashing of life means that these are definitely social nights. It no longer matters that you could stay up all night doing Karaoke on Tuesday if you wanted to and lie in bed until noon the next day, Saturday is not a night for staying in alone. It's a night for exploration, wine, good food, socialising (if possible) sex (if lucky) or for me right now, a nice little tour of Xlendi, which looks pretty dire on first arrival. However, I walked down to the seafront and drifted along the array of restaurants and up along the left side of the bay. The walk meanders over the rocks and there's a footbridge taking you over to another cliff walk up to the top where you reach a plateau. This is certainly a great place for walks, with yet another defence tower perched on the cliffs at the entrance to the long narrow passage that leads to the wider bay and the small accumulation of flats, restaurants and the odd hotel. Once I got to the top of the cliff, after crossing the bridge, I walked straight over the flat bit at the top to the sea on the other side. As I approached the edge, I was not sure what would be over it, a sheer drop perhaps, but no, it was sandstone heaven with large boulders that resembled Henry Moore sculptures perched on a soft yellow surface, in which appeared the footprints of Gulliver the giant, indelibly etched into the flat surface. The setting sun, highlighted the colour and as I snapped away with my camera, I think I had a little orgasm, so beautiful and totally unexpected was the scene. I will certainly explore more of Xlendi and its walks. I stopped and had a glass of wine at the last restaurant on the left side of the bay, perched up high, with a position and view to die for, but a British couple sitting next to me who had eaten there were not overly impressed and looking at the menu myself, I thought it rather expensive in comparison with the few I have so far tried.

I've booked two hours of riding on Monday morning, with Joe at the stables in Qala. He has a farm and menagerie of animals, including two pigs that wander around free range, along with just about everything else. I arrive at 5:30 a.m. I've not been on a horse for two years, but I want to be like HM the Queen and keep riding as long as I'm able and so at my age now, I need to get back in the saddle and ride at least twice a month. Gallops are clearly out of the question in Gozo, as are any real possibilities of even having a canter, because the terrain is just too rocky, but two hours of up and down hills, picking our way through large stones and craggy little pathways, where you most certainly needed to keep your horse awake and watching where hooves were placed, combined with the scenery, was enough for my first time back in the saddle. I would never have discovered this area and accessible walking routes without exploration on horseback or a very good map (which I'm still working on). I will however always miss the wonderful riding in England, together with the birdsong and the trees. Yet right now I think my trade-off of blue sky and constant sunshine is well worth it.

There are three riding stables on Gozo so I will check them all out and find the best horses and nicest rides and make whichever wins my 'local'. I packed my trusty Harry Hall jodhpurs which are the same ones bought for me when I was aged thirteen and yes this is a testament to Harry Hall, as they must have been washed a zillion times, but also a testament to me that they still fit forty seven years after they were purchased. So well done to both his manufacturing and my body for standing the test of time!

I've now had two lessons in my new Karate class. This class bears no resemblance at all to what I was doing in the UK – Goju Ryu karate which involves learning lots of arm and leg movements and Katas (sequenced and complex movements that are a bugger to learn). The new class is a combination of Karate moves, mixed with Judo and

Boxing and it's a workout and a half. I end the class puce in the face with hair that's soaking wet and the next day I don't have the energy to lift a mug of tea, but considering that I initially got into Karate to get fit and learn self-defence, this is a class that is the fast road to both. Its involved getting rather close up and personal with the other students and I've had my legs wrapped around a man's torso, squeezing tightly, for the first time in years! Albeit he was trying to fake strangle me and I had to manoeuvre out of the hold, which meant I was then sitting astride him, so I'm actually learning how to really fight and defend myself instead of poncing about doing arm and leg symphonies. Am trying very hard not to let sexual fantasies get out of control!

4th July, 2016

I feel a little bit guilty about the extended 'holiday mode' I'm still in after two weeks since arrival, but I'm writing this book and I've joined the Maltese Art Society and I have dropped off some of my cards to a shop that might be interested in selling them, so if I have some beach time so what? I had my first siesta today lying on my extremely comfortable sofa with the fan pointed at my nose and I dropped off for about an hour and a half. It's getting very hot because the breeze that's so far been a daily occurrence has now ceased so the heat is quite oppressive and quite honestly there's nothing to do but sleep between 1:00 and 4:00 p.m. when it really is too hot for comfort, even when you love the heat. Thankfully, it does cool down a bit at night. I shall forget the trees and remember the rain with the replacement of sun, sea, sand and …. (<u>what</u> was that other one?)

Unfortunately no breeze also equals mosquitos and I got eaten alive at the Azure window where I went earlier this evening. They are always the main drawback in any hot country and I hate the little bastards – such party poopers. Burning 'Tiger coils' does the trick if you're outside. Screens are essential here, but at least there are no cockroaches like there were in Bermuda and in the Caribbean. There

44

are not many flies either and the ones that are here are very small, not like the bulbous blue bottles you get in the UK that look as if they've been feeding off a Buffalo and then want to crap in your sugar.

6th July, 2016

There has to be some discussion regarding the traffic and the local acceptance of the driving code, the rules of which are exceedingly grey, particularly in Gozo. There's no road rage here at all, basically because everyone does just about whatever they like with regard to driving, the legalities of which are nearly always overlooked and accepted by everyone as just part of life. Speeding is rare because most of the roads are too bumpy, so most driving never exceeds 65 kph, even on the good bits of road in Gozo. People stop in the middle of the road to chat, park momentarily anywhere, without the threat of a Hitlerish Traffic Warden pouncing on them, although there are certain places you just don't park and everyone accepts that. You NEVER park in front of someone's garage door on which there is always a sign telling you it's in use day and night. In Victoria particularly, Gozitan's can often be found reversing back up a one way street in order to avoid having to drive round a one-way system that takes up a wasted five minutes of life. No entry signs on streets anywhere are not always easy to spot and there are dozens of one way streets, so tourists (which I'm not any longer) and Grannies (which I am) can often be found driving down one way streets, causing mayhem. If you do this though, you will not be cursed or have the 'dickhead' sign made at you, but a Gozitan driver will politely tell you that this is one way, so thanking them profusely, you reverse back up the road in true local tradition.

One does have to sometimes deal with the 'Boy Racers', charging about in their super charged-up cars with exhaust pipes the size of reservoir drain pipes and engines loud enough to wake the dead. They can fly past you at scary speeds and you just really wish there was a radar trap up ahead, but usually there isn't. Most of the time though these lads race about late at night, long after grannies and tired farmers have stopped cluttering up the road and gone to bed.

Horns are generally not used unless you pass a friend, or you happen to be the bread or vegetable man, in which case, the horn is peeped incessantly in order to let people know you're there and for some reason these horns are rather loud and even more intrusive than Mr Whippy on a cloudy day! One thing I do find rather odd, especially considering the outgoing friendliness of Gozitan's, is that they rarely put up a hand to say thank you when you stop to let a car pass because of parked obstacles that impinge on the right of way. I suppose it's something to do with the fact that it happens so often, it's just accepted as part of the driving culture here and it's too hot to be waving thank you a hundred times a day. I still do though, but I've not even been here a month yet, so it may dwindle.

The other thing most certainly worth mentioning is that roads very often merge into each other with no right of way markings to indicate who's meant to give way! This means that when driving you really have to have your wits about you and continually imagine that another driver is about to plough into the side of your car from either the left or right and slowing down just in case is always the order of the day. Who exactly it is that has right of way is never really known by anyone and the rule of thumb is that the one who is closer to the destination point at the meeting of the roads is the one who goes first, but you always have to approach road merges with caution just in case it's not you who is presumed to have the right of way. Very confusing and how on earth insurance companies sort out prangs of this type is beyond me!

Then there are the Lawnmowers, but no grass! Quite often in Gozo the stillness of the day or evening can be shattered by a deafening noise which turns out to be a farmer driving some kind of souped-up up lawnmower with a small trailer attached to it. These are usually full of very long canes or reeds and I'm not sure if they're bamboo or sugar cane or what they are used for, but it's a crop that is often cut when dried and clearly used for something. I wondered about this as a mode of transport and imagined that instead of cane, I could simply fill my trailer with brimming Waitrose or Lidl bags. I don't think I'll need a tax disc for the lawnmower, but will definitely require ear defenders.

This evening I walked around the narrow residential lanes of Victoria which have lots of character, though they must be oppressively hot with no breeze and traffic fumes to contend with, so I'd never want to live there. Many of the houses are old with beautiful antiquated wooden doors, with faded and peeling paint from the heat and ancient door knobs willing you to turn the handles back in time. These narrow streets are a must to explore by foot and many of them are too narrow for cars and wind around like a rabbit warren or maze, but you can't really get lost because it's just not big enough. At about 7:00 p.m. I walked up the hill and a vast number of steps to the Cittadella as I wanted to photograph it at sundown. I had been there during my holiday in May, but in the morning and the light was too harsh. Evening is the best time, though most of the attractions within it close at 5:00 p.m., so thankfully there weren't many people about. I found an absolute peach of a restaurant inside, perched up in the ramparts, with a view to die for, watching the sun set over the countryside on one side of the terrace and Victoria starting to light up far below you on the other. The food was also very good, so I shall go back there and definitely put it on the list of where to take any friends or family that come out to visit.

Right now I'm sitting out on my balcony and there's a really cool breeze and I actually feel a little chilly for the first time since I left the UK! It's a blissful respite actually. Since I arrived sixteen days ago, I have experienced 39 drops of rain. I know this because I counted the drops in the dust on the tiles on my balcony! Sixteen days of no rain, nothing but blue sky and sunshine and that's the way it is. If we had sixteen days of even a paltry 25°C in the UK, everyone would be complaining that it was too hot! Having now experienced sixteen days of around 33°C, which is too hot, I've decided that my optimum temperature is actually 24°C and when it drops to 21°C, I think it's a bit nippy! I am really looking forward to my first big thunderstorm and the view from here will be stunning, but I may have to wait a while for that, looking at the local five day forecast. There's been no proper rain for five months, so I may have a long wait.

The weather here can often be very windy especially if you're high up and the wind can last for four or five days, before dying back to a pleasant breeze. This happens quite suddenly and the sea whips up into a frenzy of white caps and the waves crash against the walls of the pavement restaurants and quite a few of them have to close. The effect of these sudden wind storms on the Mediterranean Sea, make you understand why so many migrants setting off in tiny boats, in what appears to be calm weather, end up a few hours later drowning in a sea that's turned almost instantly into a force of unimaginable terror.

10th July, 2016

I've been invited over to my building neighbour across the hall from me. Siem, a Digital Nomad, who never stays anywhere for long, is renting the flat opposite me and her Landlord and his girlfriend are out for a ten day holiday to share the flat. It is after all a 3-bed space. It turns out Edward and Sophie are the archetypal 'party animal Brits with a home abroad'. I was invited over for drinks at 6:00 p.m. and on crossing the threshold, I knew it was going to be one of those nights where I got hammered. Welcoming to the ninth degree, ready to party at the drop of a hat, we got tucked into to vino straight away. It wasn't long before a regulatory taxi was ordered to take us to Zeppi's in Qala. Vast amounts of alcohol were consumed. Edward and Sophie were very entertaining and actually just what I needed, having emigrated to a new country and not knowing anyone, I was in need of a bit of social bonding. Nothing quite did the bonding for me at that time more than a couple of British heavy drinkers to remind me of home.

The taxi driver actually turned out to be a great friend of Edward and Sophie, was Gozitan and the biggest flirt I have ever encountered. He duly drove us to Qala, dropped us off and promised to be a text away for our return to Xaghra. Said text was duly made about 10:00 p.m. and we returned somewhat pie-eyed to Rubbles Bar, where we proceeded to take a table indoors. The shots were ordered and I was already by that time embarrassingly deep into my cups. Thankfully, I'm a good drunk and tend to sing and want to dance or have meaningful conversations.

This particular evening, despite the very short distance from the Square in Xaghra to our flat on Gnien Imrick Street, Sophie, Edward et al decided to drive home in their Range Rover that had been parked on the square the whole night. For some reason I felt this was totally against the rules, so I proceeded to jog all the way from the square back to our flat, running in the middle of the road, so they couldn't overtake me or drive too fast. I set the pace with a jog at about 1:00 a.m. tight as a tick, yet still managing to maintain a steady and to be fair, very controlled jog back home, just in case they decided to speed in the short distance back to the flat. Not sure whether this feat made my hangover in the morning a little bit better, or a lot worse!

19th July, 2016

The Feast of St George has started, over which there will be a weeklong celebration and road closures in the middle of Rabat (re-named Victoria) and generally a bit more chaotic four wheel activity, but no road rage over parking, which extends like multi-coloured sections of great spider legs, filling every branch road extending from the belly of Gozo's largest tiny metropolis. I had gone off to Sannat early in the evening on Sunday to walk along the Seguna cliffs - a stunning walk at sunset, right on the edge of a very unsafe, three hundred foot drop to the ocean. I stayed a sensible four feet from the edge! I came back through Victoria, and fancied a beer. I was dressed acceptably by normal standards to go out in the evening and am still assumed to be a tourist on holiday, so it wasn't a problem, but something was definitely going on.

The women were all dressed up to the nines. Some looked as lovely as if they were off to Ascot on Ladies Day, although nobody was wearing a hat, just a selection of mostly dresses, of every shape and material you could imagine. High heels were the order of the evening. Little girls swanned around in delight in their princess and fairy dresses, treading carefully in their sparkling new shoes that they thought were as beautiful and delicate as glass slippers, yet they longed to run and dance. The men all wore their decent trousers and freshly ironed short sleeved shirts.

I managed to get myself a 'Cisc' (local beer) quite quickly considering the crowds, but all tables were taken so people were finding perches around the square wherever they could. I found a large stone, drank my beer and thought I would find out what was going on. The Feast of St George was being celebrated and there would be a procession of the band followed by numerous members of the clergy dressed superbly, bearing various highly ornate celebratory statues, wafting a bit of incense with enthusiasm and joy. The general public followed the colourful procession as the Cross was taken into the Basilica St George.

I spotted a beautiful street just off the square and found everyone outside their houses. This is where the procession began and it was a much better place than the square, so I was very glad I moved. Most of the houses are three storey and each level, apart from the ground floor, has a balcony. Those living higher up had the best view perhaps and paid their church dues by cutting up tiny squares of metallic paper as confetti, tossing them out at well-timed moments, onto the street below as the procession passed by. On the balcony to my right the women of the house enthusiastically scattered their hard work with timing and thought, for the best effect. The confetti shimmered like snowflakes in the street lights, as it danced and swirled in the breeze on its descent, leaving a trail of sparkling diamonds and colour in the street below. Everyone got it in their hair.

Back to St George and some facts I hadn't got a clue about before reading the very interesting and informative website of the Basilica St George. It's not a very sophisticated web site, but if you click on the left and read through the articles they're fascinating. St George lived around 284 to 303 AD, was born in Palestine and became known as a wonder worker for the Christian faith, at a time in history when Pagans were being particularly aggressive and gruesome to Christians. St George travelled throughout the Mediterranean and his reverence today, particularly with Roman Catholics that have links to the Eastern world, is huge. Hence why he is revered and enthusiastically honoured by the Maltese and Gozitan's very particularly and fairly unanimously. This fervour for St George stretches over many countries and the last 1,700 odd years. The Legend of the Dragon is also discussed on the website and there's a bit about a wily old Bishop in Rome having to be 'politically correct to the Church', whilst still recognising the significance to the people that this devout Christian Being had, which required formal recognition.

More of all this can be found on the Basilica website. Of course the church itself is beyond describing, as are most throughout the Maltese islands, in their grandest gestures of splendour and faith.

It can be a bit of a shock to observe huge iconography in its full display, particularly for those of Church of England/Anglican faiths, where we're just used to a bit of incense, but the Maltese and Gozitan's are particularly devout Catholics and seem to think far more about the Holy Virgin Mary than they do about the actual teachings of her Bambina Son. This is rather at odds with most of us Brits, particularly all the pomp, statues and relics that are paraded through the streets on Saints Days. The Maltese have lots of Public Holidays which are nearly all to do with religious days.

21st July, 2016

There ought to be an explanation of the Maltese/Gozitan perceptions these two sets of islanders have about each other. This of course is entirely my own opinion and I've not been here two months yet, so what do I know? Basically, they don't seem to hold each other or their respective islands in the greatest of esteem. There's a fair amount of competitiveness, though this would probably never be admitted to by either side. The Gozitan's view the Maltese as a bit too self-important and cosmopolitan for their own good and the Maltese view the Gozitan's as parochial dinosaurs preoccupied with tomatoes! Very few Maltese ever want to live in Gozo, although they do quite often holiday here, but they'd die of boredom if this was all there was. Most Gozitan's would rather die than ever contemplate living in Malta. The people of Gozo like to be called Gozitan, not Maltese and my impression is they'd be really happy if Gozo could be its own country!

The reality of animal life here, with particular regard to cats became evident to me yesterday and unfortunately it's not good. At around 1:00 p.m. I had a knock on my door from my neighbour, Siem, who asked if I liked cats. I said "of course". She said "follow me". We ducked and dived through cactus to a very rocky area to the right of our flat building. She told me she had heard a kitten mewing loudly the day before, but had not touched it, as she was told by a friend to wait for the mother cat to return and deal with her kitten. Twenty four hours later the mother had not returned and when we approached, the kitten was mewing so loudly as to only be cries for help. Feral it might have been but when I got within sight it ran into my outstretched palm desperate for help, dehydrated, hungry, frightened, and clearly feeling totally alone. I told Siem, who was flying back to Holland that night, that we couldn't possibly leave it there and I brought it up to my flat immediately and was left as the one responsible for looking after it. I checked the undercarriage and thought I saw early signs of testicles.

In a scramble of make do, we found a laundry hamper to serve as a bed when we laid it flat on the floor and dug out a cardboard box that had housed a recent purchase of a juicer, which we lay open side on the floor and lined it with newspaper and a bit of soil, for a loo. I gave him copious amounts of water via a dropper, as he was too young to know how to drink from a bowl. He did know how to eat though and did so with relish. The poor wee thing was not more than five weeks old and if we had not intervened, would have died a slow death through dehydration and abandonment. Within a few hours, he realised I was an adoptive Mummy and he clung to me with a tenacity for life. He used the cardboard loo instinctively and immediately, not once making a mistake anywhere else. He was so small and defenceless and quite utterly helpless without human intervention. Siem flew back to Holland, knowing the kitten was looked after. I prepared to spend my first night with a kitten that was still howling very loudly in the early afternoon, but by bedtime, knew it was bedtime and settled quietly and comfortably in a fluffy towel in the depths of the clothes hamper and never uttered a mew all night.

I have called him Gulliver because he had travelled from where Siem had originally found him and because his little life of just a few weeks has already been rather a journey and also, ironically, because he's so tiny, so Gulliver seemed a good name. I rang the SPCA today, but spoke to a very unsympathetic British woman who told me that basically he was now my responsibility and that they were overrun by kittens and when I asked what I was meant to do, in not so many words, but the tone was certainly there, I was told that I could just sod off. I was not impressed as this did not sound like a person concerned with the welfare of animals.

I went off this morning to find something to get rid of fleas on kittens and get two tins of decent fish cat food and some kitten milk. Gulliver is now rid of fleas but still not drinking on his own and so I'm still giving him water with the dropper I normally use to get the dregs out of my e-liquid bottles that never want to relinquish their last 2 mil of liquid. Yes, I did wash it out well – don't want the cat ingesting vanilla nicotine! I really can't keep Gulliver myself; my tenancy agreement states no pets and I have a sofa and six dining room chairs that are scratch pole heaven, with a hefty price tag for damage. My life right now is also too up in the air to be tied responsibly to any pet. Although I was quite prepared to rescue an animal in distress, I'm not able to keep him for a number of reasons, the least of which is that I don't know as yet whether I will even stay in Gozo long term and I don't want to pay for wrecked furniture that a cat kept indoors is quite likely to target for claw maintenance.

After about a week of him eating and drinking well, I decided to rather blatantly show him off, wrapped in an orange sorbet coloured towel, to the diners on the square in Xaghra tonight. Gulliver behaved like the perfect little Angel he is, but most of those who fell

54

in love were tourists. No hope there then in finding him a new loving home. If only people all over the world would simply neuter their pets – some places will do this for free, so it's not a financial thing and getting the males done costs very little anyway, whether they're cats or dogs. This would put an end to the vast numbers of unwanted kittens and puppies that never asked to be born and only require to be loved and cared for.

Thankfully people here do look after the cats, dispensing vast amounts of food at 'Feeding Stations' where the cats congregate and the more intrepid people feeding them often try to catch the cats and take them to the vets for the inevitable medical care they need, or for spaying and neutering. This is not an easy task though as the cats are feral and not keen on being touched.

Unfortunately Malta has a large number of stray dogs, as well as feral cats and although Gozo does not have many stray dogs, it has huge populations of feral cats. There are dog rescue shelters on both islands, but mostly people just feed the cats on Gozo and the dogs are caught on Malta if possible and go to rescue homes. If you want a dog or cat on either island, there is a plethora of both species desperately requiring loving homes. I eventually found a loving home for Gulliver with a lady who had another cat and a small dog.

Gulliver soon ruled the roost and it turned out he didn't have testicles so was renamed Sandra!

3rd August, 2016

After Gulliver left, I was a bit depressed. I decided a good snorkel would cheer me up so I headed off to Mgarr ix-Xini (pronounced Em garr (soft G) isheenie). This little cove is accessed via a long, bumpy and very narrow road that descends to the bay and parking area via a short extremely steep slope. At the bottom there's a beach restaurant/café with good food and tables overlooking the bay. Be warned though – it is very expensive, due to its Brangelina fame! A favourite pastime of many of the local patrons is to place bets on how many attempts it will take those leaving the beach to drive up the steep ramp. Every time some innocent and oblivious person gets ready to depart, bets are placed, based on the age and sex of the driver, as well as the make of the car. Lots of people get stuck half way up and have to reverse back down and take another run at it. Sometimes this can happen several times much to the delight of the voyeurs gambling on the driving experience of the unsuspecting participants. All bets were on with me of course and likely to be high odds, being a female of a certain age, in a very dusty hire car, but they hadn't reckoned on me driving up the steep hill from Victoria to Xaghra ten times a week, so I've had practice with road challenges. I must have both surprised and disappointed them when I ascended like a pro and hopefully crushed their misconceptions about Grannies behind wheels. Serves them right!

This is the beach and cove where Brad and Angelina filmed 'By the Sea' and I wondered if they each had a go and a bet at getting up the ramp and who might have won. In the film it doesn't really look the same at all and most of it is shot within a mock up mansion they built on the cliff, but when you go there and you see the film, it certainly shows you the enormity of what's created in the name of entertainment. Be warned though, other than the joy of seeing Gozo in a movie and spotting the local 'Extras', the film is the pits (pardon the pun) and is quite honestly one of the most boring films ever made!

9th August, 2016

I found that the purchase of a car was a bit of a Chicken and Egg situation. Renting a car long term is very expensive because of the insurance. Having a car is a necessity for me, so I decided to buy one. I trawled the Maltapark.com site and found two cars I wanted to view. I set off from home at 9:25 a.m. and an hour later I was in Mosta, which is fairly central Malta. I had no satnav or GPS though, so it took me another hour and a half to find the car place in Paolo. The roads and traffic in Malta really are a nightmare. My very old IPhone just couldn't handle the GPS download, but it really is essential in Malta. Having paid the deposit and come away with a receipt, a copy of the sellers ID card and the signed car log book, my next job was to get it insured before the transfer to me could be completed. I found out a little too late that what I also needed to do was to immediately apply for my own Maltese ID card via an application for residency. You cannot own a car without a Maltese ID Card. As soon as you have a residential address, apply for your ID card. This can be done at the E-residency part of the Government Offices on Independence Square in Victoria.

I rang the Accountant again and he said that the fastest way to make the application was by a declaration of self-sufficiency, not self-employment, as the latter would take several months. I went into the Office for E-residency in Victoria armed with a year's bank statements, copies of my health and medical insurance and my passport. You need to be able to prove that you have a regular decent monthly income, or have at least €14,000 in your bank account and that you're covered for any medical bills should you need hospital treatment. At the time of arrival, I did have UK private health insurance, but you can also buy it here and it's cheaper than the UK. After Brexit, this is quite probably an essential part of the residency application. Within forty five minutes I had my application done. The actual card will follow in a couple of weeks. I am now officially a resident of Gozo. I can change the status to self-employed at a later date when my artwork and belongings arrive and I either start to sell my work, or want to apply for a job here. It was a painless exercise that I'd been dreading for nothing.

When buying a car either on Malta Park (a great website for all things sold), or through a garage dealer, do thoroughly check everything on the car and make sure it works – don't assume anything. Cars on these islands are subjected to a rough life and bits wear out and drop off. If you're on a budget like I was, things are likely to be faulty, but the good news is that they don't cost a lot of money to fix if you can find the right mechanic.

20th August, 2016

It's another one of those Saturday nights – lots on – the Nadur Wine Festival and another Festa at Zebugg, but sadly I can't go to any of them as the back lights on my car are non-existent. No, I did not check the lights when I bought my car, which I should have done. Check EVERYTHING when buying a car in Malta! The water doesn't work for the windshield wipers either, despite the tank being full. I've met a mechanic working for himself and recommended by my neighbour. The mechanic has a Boxer dog which I thought was a very good omen. He looked over the car briefly which is also missing quite badly and not idling correctly. I have to ring him on Monday and in between fishing, which seems to be his main priority in life, he will fit in my car for some repairs. So not being able to attend the wine festival which I had wanted to go to, I decided to have my own wine festival on my balcony, play some music and write some more. It's a hot sultry night with no breeze at all and the day has been hellish hot. The sea is as flat as a pancake. As a side note, I got all the repairs done on my car for €35! I know for sure they wouldn't even have opened the bonnet for that amount in England!

21st August, 2016

We need to bear in mind that the Maltese nation as a whole love the Brits and adored having the Royal newlyweds living near Valletta back in 1949. The Maltese helped us and we helped them during WWII. Unfortunately Malta was heavily bombed during the war and many beautiful old buildings were flattened. We have a very special relationship with each other. There are British phone boxes on the island. English is their spoken language after Maltese and as two different and separate nations, British and Maltese get along and adore each other perhaps more than any other two nations in the World. I have a tiny feeling that a lot of this may be down to HM the Queen and Prince Philip and their wonderful time in Malta during the early years of their marriage before HRH Princess Elizabeth became HM the Queen.

22nd August, 2016

It feels good to be an official resident, driving my own little red Maltese plated car, which I collected today. Sitting out on my balcony, after a long walk around Xaghra this evening, I can't help but think how lucky and happy I am. Of course I've no idea what the winter will be like yet, in terms of how cold or wet it gets and whether it will be so quiet and closed up that I get a bit bored, but right now, it's total bliss. The Cicadas are chirping and little Pipistrelle bats are flying around the lights, catching moths on the wing. There's been a little cloud cover over the last few days and it's not been quite so hot, but still no rain. Apparently rain is more likely in late September as thunderstorms start, but proper winter is the first few months of the year and traditionally the wettest. Having acclimatised to the heat, I probably will feel very cold in winter, but I've brought my thermal vests, though sadly my electric blanket and duvet are tucked up in storage. It will be great though to get out and hike during dry winter days and really explore the island on foot. The light is really clear in winter too, so daytime photography will be much better. I feel right now that probably, I will love Gozo in the quiet respite of winter, more than I do in the heat and the hot bustle of summer.

26th August, 2016

I've been out doing lots of walking around Xaghra during the evenings, covering about 3 to 4 km per walk. It's easy to get lost as the place is a rabbit warren of one way streets, dead ends and lanes beckoning you to explore. The fingers of this town branch out over a very wide area and several different valleys, the views being marvellous, if you happen to stumble across the right road to view them on. You can't really get lost because the place is on the top of a hill so if you at least stay on the hill and keep wandering around, you'll hopefully find your way back to the square and the impressive church. You can however also find yourself walking around in circles and taking turns that are actually the opposite of where you want to go. I tried driving around to see if I could familiarise myself with the place more easily, but believe me, walking is much easier. I finish my walk, which I admit, is usually at a fairly cracking pace, wet with sweat, even in the cool of the evening. I look forward to winter walks when it's cold.

Xaghra is gearing up for its Festa on the 8th of September – the last one on the island. Preparation started today with the square being shut down to traffic and cars waiting whilst lights were being strewn across the streets via a cherry picker taking up space in the middle of the road. An elaborate, candle-lit mass was held this evening outside the front of the church, with about 200 chairs in place, microphone booming, Clergy in full regalia, bells ringing and the Latin liturgy in full flow, much to the delight of the dining tourists in the scattered restaurants around the square, overlooking the church. I sat and had a glass of wine at 'Rubbles Bar' (fast becoming my local) and went for my walk a little later, setting off at about 8:15 p.m. instead of my usual 7:15 p.m. It's very humid tonight without a breath of air. Rumour has it that a big storm is just south of Malta and may hit Gozo tonight. Not a chance I fear – no such luck! I actually crave some rain and I never thought I would ever say that. In fact I crave a mother of a thunderstorm, with great big black menacing clouds, cracks of thunder and the sky lighting up in vivid shades of purple and bright white light. It certainly is eerily quiet weather right now, so not sure if it could be a build-up or simply a let-down for a few days of breezeless weather.

In the evenings, the locals all sit around outside their doors, on their porches if they have one, or on the pavement if they don't. Benches are scattered everywhere and often occupied in the evenings. Because of the heat, naturally the coolest place to be is outside, particularly with the houses in the villages that have no view or access to any breeze that may be going. Consequently, the evening gathering of locals sitting out on the street, whether individually, as couples, friends or entire families is a nightly routine. When walking past, they always look up and the polite and expected local greeting is a simple nod of the head. Saying "Bonsoir" is just too exhausting for everyone (rather like putting your hand up to say thanks when driving) and nobody wants to have their conversation interrupted, or be disturbed from their contemplative silence, but a nod is essential good manners. You certainly don't do the UK thing and sail by ignoring people.

30th August, 2016

In the run up to the Festa, the square has been closed to traffic now for four days and various activities have been going on in the evening. The Festa itself is not until the 8th of September, but preparation and build-up are clearly key! Tonight was a real treat. I had set off at 7.30 p.m. for my usual walk around the village, which is still like a rabbit warren to me and I constantly get lost and can't find where I want to get to. I greatly desire a proper map of Xaghra, but fear I must resort to a hopefully up to date satellite image on Google Earth. As I rounded the home stretch towards the square, I was by then gasping for a glass of wine and it didn't take me long to realise that something else was going on tonight. Apparently the new Priest for the main church was being welcomed and here again, women were dressed up for Hello Magazine shoots, chairs were laid out, this time on the sides of the square and the energy of the place was buzzing. As per usual, I was in shorts, T-shirt, no make-up and exceedingly sweaty, so once again underdressed for the occasion.

It actually got slightly chilly tonight and was cloudy yesterday and today, so the weather is on the change. Summer is thankfully almost over and only the last few tourists remain. However the end of summer here doesn't mean the end of hot or warm sunny days and apparently the beach in December is still a possibility, but we are hopefully coming to the end of the relentless heat and blue sky without the wonderful decoration of cloud. September can be the worst in terms of humidity though, but there might be the odd thunderstorm which is a welcome respite. Even though sunscreen will always be required for me when I'm outside, it will be wonderful when it will be cool enough to enjoy the days out walking, marvelling at the rain, which to be fair I've missed a bit. I'm really looking forward to once again wearing jumpers and maybe even thermal vests. Three months of winter will suit me very well I think, having a gradual cooling down of temperature, a lower count of sunny days, interspersed with wind, cloud and thunderstorms, will be a welcome change. Winter doesn't really start until the end of December, though January, February and March are tough - high humidity, rain and wind that's cold enough to make it feel raw, but I can put up with that, when it's followed by eight months of great weather. Or so I hope.

14th September, 2016

I have three bedrooms in this flat which is actually much too large for me, but hey ho I cope. I was not prepared however for the green growth that surprised me when looking through my wardrobe for a skirt to wear for a change, fancying my black layered one, I opened the wardrobe to find it covered in green mould. I mean my skirt had become its own Eco-system – it was almost moving. I investigated further into the wardrobe and actually everything was covered in a green furry mould that resembled something out of an Attenborough documentary. Oh bugger – I need to do a big wash don't I? Dehumidifiers are a very necessary part of the furniture here and I could have kicked myself for selling off mine for a couple of quid. The humidity is in the 80% range most of the year and in winter that equals cold damp that is a haven for mould spores.

5th October, 2016

I found out about a jam session taking place at Xaghra Lodge every other week with musicians just taking along their instrument of choice and having a great old sing and play along. It was open to anyone to join in. It was held in a huge beautiful old Gozitan house, with an enormous enclosed courtyard at the back, set up with tables and chairs amongst the trees and cicadas, with strategic lighting and a great atmosphere. Our hosts were the indomitable Dave, who wore a huge gold chain around his neck and his Russian Ukulele playing wife, who ran the bar and unfortunately I've forgotten her name. It was a sort of mini hotel, very much of the kind you would imagine in the Hotel California song. I actually thought the world of Dave and always arrived a little bit early so I could have a chat with him. He had a heart of gold, was as Essex as anyone could be, but he had lived a very interesting life, loved horse and dog racing and for me it was just a treat to talk to a man who had so much to tell me about his experience of life.

Anyone could contribute to the evening's line up and I sang a few songs to the music accompaniment that was so willingly obliged. Of course those who lived in the village could get quite tight by the time it ended, always at midnight. It was a magical place. There were clear signs of the building needing money spent for repair, but it remains one of my best memories of early Xaghra days. There is somewhere out in the ether of the internet a photo of me singing along with Stefano, a well-known professional local musician, originally from Italy.

21st December, 2016

This is moving day – my six month tenancy is up and it's time to move on. I'm looking for the right longer term home, but in the meantime I have found a flat on the promenade between Marsalforn and Qbajjar, right in front of the children's playground. I am only moving 'the stuff on my back' i.e. what I came here with as excess baggage, so manage to do this in two car loads of stuff. I didn't want to take out another term after my six month tenancy expired, quite honestly due to the mould eco-system within the flat, but also because I realised that paying €600 a month for this flat was rather a high rent for what was actually available. The new flat is in a small holiday apartment block called Blue Waters, thirty feet from the sea, on a quiet part of the road between Marsalforn to the Salt Pans, but within an easy 10 minute walk of Marsalforn and its winter life. The flat owners are delightful and the top floor is occupied by a single Swedish party animal of about my age, whose name is Louise. We soon made friends and became drinking buddies and regulars at the Glassbox and both loved to sing on their Open Mic nights.

1st January, 2017

I can't actually remember much about New Year's Eve. Louise and I soon became friends and both enjoyed having a companion to go out with at the weekend. We usually went to the Glassbox. On NYE Stefano was playing and we sang with him and there was dancing. There were some other locals we knew from various places around the Globe. We got tight as ticks and staggered home. I never ended up going to bed, but wrote on my computer and called my sons in a time zone hours before mine in terms of clocks. At about 5:30 a.m. I thought, why bother going to bed! At 6:30 a.m. I was swimming in the warm water of Xweni Bay. The air temperature was perishing so the water felt like a warm bath. I had walked down as I was actually still quite pickled, but actually it was just what I needed to start off my New Year. I had the place to myself – the whole ocean, the beach, the morning.

It was one of the greatest starts to New Year's Day I have ever had and the swim in the energy of the ocean sorted out my own vibration and hangover. I couldn't believe how warm the water felt. I had a little snorkel. I floated and looked up at the clouds on the new day and I gave thanks for everything. Yeah, it was an amazing start to 2017 and I felt it was going to be a great year for me.

28th January, 2017

In the five weeks I've been in Marsalforn I've met more people than the entire time I've been in Gozo, most of whom have been met at the local pub, called 'Electra' which stays open all day, mostly all year, for the locals as a drinking hole and meeting place. The vibe is friendly and laid back and most of the time, even in January, you can still sit outside in sunshine, albeit more fleeting moments of. Everyone brings an assortment of jumpers, coats and scarves which are continually put on and taken off according to the whims of the sun and the clouds. When delighting us with its presence the sun is warm and welcoming and if there's no wind, only a lightweight jumper is required, even in January. Apparently though it's been the coldest winter in Malta for 68 years – a new record that I instinctively knew they could put down entirely to me, ditto the fact that it has rained a huge amount this winter. I have this effect on the weather around the World wherever I go. If you want to get rid of a drought, invite me for three or four months - it will rain!

The great thing about the winter is that most of the restaurants and bars are closed, so the ones that are open are inhabited by local people so you get to meet far more residents in the sparsely populated island in winter than you do when it's heaving with tourists. Sunday afternoons are spent in idle conversation, meeting friends and friends of friends, expats and locals alike – the big soup of acceptance simmers fruitfully in the winter of Gozo.

The weather has been challenging through most of January, with cold wind, sometimes the odd bit of hail, raging tormented seas and mostly everyone shivering without the benefit of reasonably economical, but more importantly efficient methods of heating their homes. Wood burners are essential here if at all possible. Unless you are well off, few houses have central heating, because most of the time it's simply not needed, except for when it really is, but the problem is that modern houses built here have no insulation and no radiators. Many are built with walls exposed to the elements and they are not cozy homes. January and February are really cold and damp and feel exceedingly unpleasant. Most of the time it's warmer outside than it is inside. Layers are an essential part of life, as is an electric blanket or several hot water bottles. Bedtime for me is frequently about 7:30 p.m. with my Kindle, simply because it's the only place I can be warm. Layers needed for daytime indoors; tights under trousers, thick knee length socks, leather shoes or boots, a thermal vest, shirt, lightweight jumpers x 2, thick heavy jumper and scarf. That's indoors and really necessary if you have no heat. Gloves are also sometimes required, but this frightful cold might only last a week and then it can be warm enough again to tempt the intrepid to go for a swim, before it might disintegrate again into the cold you came here to escape from. A wood burner could solve my problems – either that or the nonchalant glance at a €120 a month electric bill.

4th February, 2017

I walked into 'Electra' on a cold blustery day because I just needed the energy of people around me. I have come to understand over the years that living as a single person (though usually having a dog for a companion) and not having much of a social life, that actually being around people can have a huge effect on my own wellbeing. I might not have to connect with them, but I can survive any feelings of loneliness if I immerse myself in the energy of others for an hour or so. However on this particular day, I had not reckoned on finding myself in conversation with a wiry man who looked a little off his head, attached to a dog called Harry. He was an artist, quite revered and famous on the island, so it's no wonder we connected, found lots to talk about and Harry and I got on immediately. Harry's owner was clearly an old flirt, a man after my own heart in terms of his preferred genre of entertainment. Philosophical conversations were de'rigeur and I thought his art was truly amazing, him being an abstract artist. He is a well-known figure of an ancient local family and a character I feel very lucky to have met.

The winter weather and waves were dramatic and inspiring, especially for the photographers on the island. I did my share of standing around waiting and in fact waited about fifteen minutes to get this particular shot of the waves breaking over the stacked-up restaurant chairs.

22nd February, 2017

I've been searching for the right house for a long term let, somewhere I can import all my stuff, still sitting in storage in the UK, finding a long term home where I can stay and be happy. I found a small Estate Agent in Victoria and a delightful man called Michael who had the most beat up heap of a car I have ever seen for an Estate Agent. Michael had shown me quite a few places but he rang me early one morning and told me about a place that was about to come onto the market. As we drove towards Gharb, he commented that he felt he bad he had not managed to find me anywhere thus far and I said "well maybe this one will be it Michael". Indeed it was. I fell in love within stepping over the threshold and knew this was where I wanted to live. I took the lease from the 1st March, 2017 and was delighted with it.

10th March, 2017

Gozo lost its most iconic view of nature on Wednesday 8th of March at 9:40 a.m. with the complete annihilation of the Azure Window at Dwjera. Everyone throughout the Maltese islands and all those who've known this particular spot, are grieving at the loss of a splendid sculpture created by the genius of Nature. There is no small part left behind in anything but memories now and what we see through recorded images. No more live vision and inevitable instinctive wonder. Of course the abstract, final resting place of all that rock, will provide a new landscape and habitat to an underwater world.

The loss now has been a shock for all of us, apart from those aware of the more serious problems with the fragility of the structure under the sea. Most of us never thought it would happen yet. With the sad diagnosis of what was happening below the water line, as well as the crack on the top of the bridge, it was made illegal to walk over it, or indeed get too close to it, in November. This was done with large signs and lots of media coverage and a hefty fine levied if the warning was ignored. Prior to November, tourists regularly walked across. I don't think I could have ever done that myself, being terrified of heights, but I consider this quite a close call in stopping people JUST IN TIME! If it had happened after a summer storm, without the ban being in place, a great many tourists would have been all over the site and if it had collapsed, would have landed in the sea, crushed by falling rock. We have to give thanks for that not being the case. The moment was chosen well. I don't believe the divers and geologists giving the 'any day' prognosis, probably imagined that day would be quite so soon or so utterly complete either. Above the waterline it's as if it never existed. Not even some lonely spike of the outer pillar to remind us of its former glory – nothing at all is also rather a shock. I would never have thought for a moment when I first set eyes on it in May, 2016 that I would not have the pleasure of looking at it ever again, less than a year later.

I have been many times in the nearly nine months of living here. The best time to visit is certainly in winter when everything is closed up. Days when there are no tourist stalls open, no buses. Early in the morning, with the stars starting to fade in the lightening dawn. Certainly the only time you might be lucky enough to be alone. Evening with the sun setting in the background, when the sea is as smooth as glass, then the jewel of the Azure Window was at its best. In the warm evenings, you would get quite a few people to watch the sunset. Everyone wished it could just be the arch and them. There were the spectacular wave days when the wind whipped up the waves, which hurled themselves at the rocks, screaming with spray in the strength and power of the sea. Days spent at the mercy of the wind and all the raging it brings, amongst days spent in calm contemplation peacefully at rest, for a little while.

The inevitable interest and resulting economic development, was perhaps no longer the cloak Mother Nature wished to wear. It certainly was not an attractive one. Large numbers of people visiting sites all over the world, becoming an opportunity for making bucks everywhere. No country seems to be immune. People visiting equals money to be made. Buses offer frequent visits to Dwjera all day. There are several Ice cream stands, a small shop for postcards, facilities, vendor's selling clothing, jewellery, food, woodwork and leather and there's very good parking. The inland sea, a great shallow

70

and calm little bay with cafes, boat trips and small beach front homes nestling by the water, sits below a restaurant that serves reasonable food. The Window was an icon around the World, high on the most photographed list. Because of its spectacular beauty, we all spoiled it in a way. Who out of any of us would not have preferred to quietly come across it on a peaceful coastal walk, feeling very lucky to have found it without its tourist accompaniments? The Azure Window was a jewel in the art of nature and we all feel bereft of it. A very unfortunate loss for Malta as a country and heart wrenchingly sad for everyone sharing the island of Gozo that hosted its creation, vision and final transformation.

16th April, 2017

I decided it was time for a dog in my life again. Yes I know I could have gone to the rescue home and if there's ever a next time, I shall do this, but right now I want a puppy and I need a small dog that will need lots of walking. I really wanted a Border terrier, but there were no breeders on the islands and to bring a puppy from the UK would both be very expensive and also bypass my reasons for wanting a puppy – to be the replacement Mummy from 8 weeks old. You can't internationally transport a puppy before 16 weeks and I wanted to be a surrogate Mummy from the first possible age of leaving the natural Mother. I have this thing about bringing up a puppy, but eventually after giving up on a Border terrier, I found a Jack Russell breeder in Malta who had a litter of pups born today. I decided to buy one. He arrived eight weeks later delivered by car to Gozo, sitting on the lap of a Priest.

I've never had a small dog before, always preferring large breeds, like Mastiff's, Boxer's, or Great Danes and puppyhood was rather challenging with this small bundle of fur that zipped about like fly. Having a puppy and keeping it indoors until all shots are administered was certainly a nightmare. Thankfully I did have a large outdoor terrace, but housetraining was achieved using Puppy Pads and we managed. Hamish McAllister is what he clearly told me his name was,

71

so Hamish he became. He'd obviously lived in Glasgow in a past life and was a right little bruiser in those early months. I had to assert my position as top dog and it was a tough battle that left me in tears, but he relented his position and realised I was boss. I couldn't live without him now and we have been best friends ever since, but those early months without a proper 'wee and poo garden' were pretty horrendous.

4th May, 2017

The month of my birthday. I have this puppy that I can neither leave nor take anywhere with me, so I decide to have a party at home. I am after all living in this most beautiful old house with an ancient manger in my sitting room reminding me of days gone by. I lit candles and decided to teach my puppy the art of dancing. He certainly seemed to enjoy the music, since I'm not into heavy metal or anything likely to offend the ears. I tried to teach him to dance, but mostly just enjoyed being with him in a candle lit beautiful room and I felt extremely fortunate to be living here.

The strange thing was that when I was here on holiday a year ago staying at Ta'Kalminja B & B, I saw the house I'm now living in and thought "I'd really like to live there". So you see, we can manifest things we want and desire, sometimes it's only a fleeting feeling, or so we imagine, but thoughts and emotions come into being and they certainly did for me with this house.

22nd July, 2017

Hamish is just adorable and in another four weeks, he can go outside into the big wide World after he's had his final vaccination. There is a very nasty mosquito here and throughout the Mediterranean, called the Sand Fly. They carry a disease called Leishmaniosis and if humans are bitten by a Sand Fly there can be serious consequences if it's not looked at quickly. Dogs however can't ever recover from this and have to be on permanent medication if they get this disease. They get extremely thin no matter how much they eat. They should be vaccinated annually against it, but because the shot isn't 100% effective, they should also wear a Scalibor collar specifically for Sand Flies. The trouble with this particular species of mosquito is that it's very tiny, so you can't see them. They come out just after sunrise for a couple of hours and again just before sunset. You're pretty safe in the heat and strong sun, but they are around most of the year and reside in rural areas, caves, rock walls etc. They are called Sand Flies because of their colour, NOT because they live on the beach! Since many of the villages have rural areas with rock walls, fields and places these little buggers live, you can be bitten sitting on your own terrace in the evening, so cover up, use insect repellent and Tiger coils to repel them. I put Citronella oil on Hamish's fur too as a triple precaution if he's coming out with me in the evening.

My new house is much cooler than the flat I had in Xaghra because the downstairs used to be an old stone barn, complete with feeding manger. The stone it's built from is soft and sandy and exceedingly thick, so it keeps in the heat in winter and keeps in the cool in summer. This stone however needs regular hoovering because sandy salts are expelled from the stone, making it look furry after six weeks and the residue frequently falls onto the floor, so wall hoovering is a monthly chore in the old stone houses. It's as hot as hades outside and I have to admit this is much hotter than I had imagined it would be. The sky goes from a beautiful azure blue to the white blindness of mega heat and it's not comfortable. We are spending our days with the shutters closed, sitting between hard working fans. Air conditioning here is as necessary as food and thank goodness I have it in my bedroom.

I've booked my first Exhibition here for my work, most of which is all done and is due to arrive imminently, along with all my furniture and beloved stuff. The Exhibition will be held in the main Gallery Hall of the Cittadella, in December, 2018. I had to get on the waiting list as there is no charge to use the space and it's an incredible place to have an Exhibition. I will add some photographic work, done here in Gozo, but sadly I've not done any painting whilst here because I simply haven't had a suitable place for a studio.

16th September, 2017

I shall soon be re-united with all my stuff, packed up before the Brexit vote and not seen for well over a year. A mini crane has been hired (called a Lifter) and this is considered the normal way to deliver furniture here because of so many flats and balcony access being the easiest or sometimes only option of delivery. My house has three floors so the lifter will make life much easier than lugging stuff up flights of stairs. The removal lorry is due to arrive in about two hours. Hamish will spend the time in his large wire dog crate that was initially bought for an English Mastiff, so it's exceedingly roomy for a Jack Russell.

The house is now awash with boxes of stuff and I look upon them with trepidation. How have I still got so much stuff after my huge sale and clear out in the UK? I really must have been a male Bower Bird in a previous life. Hamish is not quite sure what to think and after initially being a tiny bit scared, he now thinks the boxes are giant Lego bricks in which to hide behind and have the occasional wee. Trying to house train a puppy without a proper garden is quite difficult, but to be fair he does usually head for the 'Puppy Pad'. It's wonderful however to see my furniture again and I'm very thankful that my Landlord took away his furniture that I no longer needed this morning in order that there was room for mine. This had been agreed at the start of my tenancy and some Landlords are willing and able to move furniture out to make way for the tenants own, provided they have another house to place it in. Thankfully, my Landlord has half a dozen rental properties so it wasn't a problem. Furniture cannot be stored in a garage here because it's just too damp, so never presume they will move things out unless you specifically ask prior to signing the lease.

I start ravaging boxes and unpacking stuff I haven't seen for ages, some of which were a happy reunion, other bits I wondered why on earth they had been kept. I'm going to need to have another sale before I move this lot anywhere else I thought. By 5:00 p.m. I was exhausted and opened a bottle of wine and retreated to my shady terrace on the top floor to play with Hamish, who had been ignored for most of the day. It will be absolute Heaven to sleep on my own Vi-Spring mattress tonight.

26th September, 2017

The unpacking has all been done, pictures hung, things placed strategically around for the best interior design effect. I always feel this is the best part of moving – the display of one's collectables and the making of a new nest – yup that bloody Bower Bird again for sure.

Thankfully the weather is beginning to cool off. We've had a huge thunderstorm and a very decent amount of rain. It was so welcome after months of dry and searing heat. The humidity has dropped a little too, so a walk with Hamish this evening should be pleasurable for the first time. I've also signed up for my first 'Exciting Hike' with John, via Meetup. We are meeting tomorrow at 11:00 a.m. and are walking through the valley at Mgarr-ix-Xini and will be exploring the old Water Tower, abandoned long ago.

27th September, 2017

There were seven of us on the walk, including John. I left Hamish at home because it's a three hour hike – too far for a young puppy. We set off through the valley and rocks at a steady pace. There's some scrambling up over rocks which was relatively easy and I couldn't help marvel at being on a walk I would never have found alone. John checks out all his walks with the precision of an Army Officer scouting for safe ground and he also gets the necessary permissions from the farmers and landowners, over whose property John often leads his motley crew of intrepid hikers. The Water Tower was incredible and very scary with a huge, deep gaping hole in the centre that was not by a long stretch made safe. Get too close to the edge and you would tumble to your death, but it was a photographer's paradise if you're into building decay, graffiti, contrast and general abandonment. Thankfully, we all had enough common sense to not get too close to the edge, so it was perfectly safe and could be enjoyed for what it was. We stopped for our packed lunch on the cliffs above the tower and by the end of the hike, I was puce in the face and sweaty again and thoroughly exhausted, but what fun it had been. I will most certainly try to do all these hikes as they are varied in scenery and difficulty and I feel sufficiently goat like to consider I could manage any of them. They will give me the opportunity to see parts of the island I would never do otherwise and also to meet other residents, as few of John's hikers are tourists.

My next walk was done a week later through the Mistra Rocks and this time it was just John, me and another British artist and long term resident called Sarah. This hike is the most difficult one out of all of them and yet is the most remote and totally incredible. It was the nearest I got to actual rock climbing as we scrambled up and down over rocks, into caves, following paths that only the most daring of mountain goats would attempt to escape a predator. Exciting it certainly was and there were a few times where John was pulling me by the hand to help me ascend, whilst Sarah behind me was pushing my butt upwards. I was after all the oldest of the three of us and had not done this hike before. I kept thinking about how impressed my sons would be seeing me do this. I was utterly exhausted at the end of it, but felt a huge sense of achievement and was very proud of myself. Beware though, this hike is generally not recommended for anyone who's a granny, is unfit or has bad knees!

28th October, 2017

The weather is now gorgeous and the island is getting green again after regular rainfall. It's now quite chilly at night and jumpers are required again. The days vary from being sunny and about 24 degrees, yet now with lovely puffy white clouds decorating the azure blue background. I welcome them back with open arms. I feel the constant blue or white skies of summer for four months get a little boring. The light is starting to soften to that hue which beckons photographers out. Most of the tourists have now gone home and the ones left are keen walkers. It feels wonderful to be able to go outside during the day, to be living as a human being again, instead of as a mole cooped up indoors in the shady darkness trying to keep cool.

Hamish is now great off the lead and charges about and off ahead of me, yet always comes back to check I'm still there. This is a very good sign for a six month old puppy – it's never good when they have enough confidence to wander off without their Mummy! I'm taking him everywhere with me and of course everyone wants to stop and say hello because he's so adorable. This is very good training and he's really enjoying the loves and cuddles from children. He's also getting used to having to sit quietly whilst I read my book, have a glass of wine or lunch. I still don't know many people, so I am a bit lonely, but thankfully absorbing the energy of everyone around me when I'm out during the day seems to be enough to keep me sane. I'm welcomed like a regular at Gharb Rangers though and do see other locals there for chats and Hamish is welcomed too. I've tried to compete with Dave's vape clouds, but decided there was no point trying to invade this male dominated new sport. Vaping in the male domain seems to have become a replacement challenge for longest Willie/can pee furthest, to who has the heaviest tank and who has the biggest, most dense cloud. Dave is very clearly the modern Champion.

Christmas, 2017

I decided to buy at the huge cost of €50, a proper Christmas tree and I've decorated the house. It was time to celebrate and have a proper Christmas. I've been invited to some friends in the village on Christmas Eve for dinner. They are wealthy Expats who've been here for about twenty years. Their house is my dream home – an old house, complete with an original Mill in their sunken sitting room.

The house and décor are divine and it was a delight to be there. My friends were gracious hosts and the evening was a traditional Christmas Eve for hubby who is not English, but his wife is. Also invited were their delightful neighbours, also of mixed nationalities, so it was a lovely collection of cultures and opinions. The table was laid to perfection and Christmas splendour and the atmosphere delightfully Christmassy. The food, in true Polish tradition was basically fish of every kind you could imagine, accompanied by great wine and huge amounts of Vodka! Yes, as usual, I got pickled, but so did a couple of others (though maybe not quite as much as me, not being used to spirits of any kind.) Conversation flowed, candles eventually burned down and it was time to weave my way the 500 yards or so I had to walk to get home and into 'ma pit'. Consequently I did not rise too early on Christmas Day and a cooked breakfast was consumed with relish, rather than having lots of presents to open. Hamish had a sausage cooked especially for him.

Despite having made a few friends here now, I'm generally happy being at home with just Hamish and I'm quite happy to spend Christmas Day and New Year's Eve tucked away in our beautiful home. Going out last night though made a big difference to my Christmas and I don't feel so isolated and alone.

Christmas is a time of huge celebration in Malta and Gozo with lots on to look at and participate in if you so desire. The Bethlehem Village in Ghajnseilem is well worth a visit, with everyone involved in the display dressed up in the clothing of over 2000 years ago, donkeys, sheep, goats and chickens brought in to add to the atmosphere. The Inn and stable where Jesus was born, faithfully recreated and carols being sung by local choirs made it all very festive and charming. The Church is obviously in its full regalia at Christmas and processions of icons, bells ringing, singing and a combination of solemnity and joy are there for anyone who wants to join in.

26th March, 2018

I realise it has been about three months since writing my book and diary basically because I've just been getting on with life, though doing actually what I'm not quite sure. Photography has played a big part and I've explored Victoria at night and really got to know my village and the island. I've made some treks to the other side of the island and the village of Qala and even ventured out in the evenings occasionally to Zeppi's the local 'It bar' in that village which has live music every weekend. I've joined a pilates class here in the village and I'm thinking about my Exhibition in December and starting to gather photographs I want to have printed and framed.

I still go to Marsalforn sometimes on a Sunday and have lunch at Otters, my favourite place because it's so close to the sea. I can simply sit there and either read my Kindle or contemplate life, watching the waves crash to the shore. I can have two glasses of wine with a meal and not worry about driving home and being stopped. This makes life here so much more pleasant. The staff all know Hamish and adore him. I bump into people I know quite often and sometimes join them. I am however not really going out at night anymore, but retreating to my nest after evening walkies and going to bed quite early. Although I am doing a few social things, I'm in a kind of rut and life seems to have ceased somewhat for me. Hamish and I are greatly enjoying our walks though.

17th April, 2018

I found a new road towards the coast, not far from home, that took us past a firework factory. There were danger signs which initially I was put off by, but after a few weeks thought I would investigate. This is a road almost opposite the tiny Chapple called San Dimitri. Arriving at the entrance of the factory there was a small shrine for some men who had lost their lives after a horrendous explosion. You see, the gunpowder stores on the islands of Malta and Gozo could feasibly, I suppose, alarm NATO, or maybe not, but they can explode at the wrong moment and people can die. We kind of scooted by because of the warning, but that road leads us down to the paved road that eventually shows you the second rock window. It's nowhere near as magnificent as the Azure Window was, but is certainly worth a view and the walk along the coast road is wonderful. I ended up meeting the owner of that factory, a lovely man called Tony, in the Gharb Rangers, who filled me in on the business of fireworks on the island.

20th June, 2018

I'm beginning to get a little depressed about life here and feeling a tiny bit bored. Gharb feels a little dull and I don't really have enough to occupy my days. I can't paint anything because I will ruin the walls and I really feel the need to express myself in a place that is not going to worry about flying blobs of white spirit mixed with oil paint, or huge blobs of acrylic landing on the walls or the floor. I feel a bit restless and I'm really hating the heat which has got beyond acceptable once again. Gharb has some lovely residents and I've made contact with people that are great fun, but the trouble is they're all married and as a single woman I'm kind of feeling a bit adrift.

28th August, 2018

The shite hits the fan big time in that my finances have been cut substantially by the results of Brexit and my time in this house has to come to an end. It feels as though my World has been turned upside down and I don't know what to do. I most certainly need to give up this house and find somewhere to rent for half what I'm paying now. I can do nothing about it. Money cannot be received where money is not there to be earned. I keep my fingers crossed for my Exhibition in four months, but I know I need to find somewhere else to live.

5th September, 2018

Of course I need to have another sale of goods – huge amounts of stuff that I no longer need. I wondered how on earth I had accumulated so many things that I didn't require anymore. A hoarder I'm not, but life has taught me that the moment you get rid of something, you're going to need it about a month later. Nevertheless, I was relentless in my discarding of belongings I hadn't used for over a year, or things that I really wasn't that bothered to be without. I occupied the pavement outside my house on the perfect weekend of the kite flying competition at the St Dimitri Chapel, so there were hundreds of cars passing by seeing vast amounts of my possessions prostituting themselves on the pavement. I did quite well in terms of what I got rid of and made a buck or two as well.

27th October, 2018

I moved across the island to Qala today with a great local team of removers and of course the inevitable lifter that was the only means of delivery for a second floor flat. It was all done and dusted in three hours. My part of course took about five days. Qala turned out to be just what I needed to boost my mood and social life. Having such a vibrant pub literally on my doorstep, filled with people wanting conversations of meaning and depth makes me feel I've landed in my element and Gozo is once more appealing to me. There are new walks here after all. I already know a few people in the village and I'm soon welcomed as a member of the Qala/Zeppi's community. It is both invigorating and exhausting at the same time. There are serious conversations about life, politics, island life, Society as a whole, much laughter and a general communing of dogs, led and kept entirely in line by Zappa, the ancient resident Patriarch.

1st December, 2018

My Exhibition has started. Everything looks amazing and I'm very proud of my paintings and photography that now hangs on the walls in this most ancient and beautiful of spaces. I have a Private View night arranged, with catering of canapes and plenty of vino. I know enough people in Gozo now to invite a bunch of them to the opening night – about thirty five friends. Just about all of them turn up and I do sell eight pieces of work, but it tended to be my lower priced pieces and so I only broke even on my costs. December however is not the best time to exhibit because there are no tourists around at this time, so all sales are dependent on locals. I did however find two fans of my work who have become huge collectors. It started tonight with their purchase of two of my works.

Over the next year Joanna and Nicholas bought more and more of my paintings and photographs, to the extent that their flat now resembles my own private gallery in Qala, with about fourteen of my works hanging on their walls. I'm exceedingly grateful for their patronage and if anyone in Gozo wants to view my work, you will have to contact them!

Unfortunately the Cittadella database of people interested in art that I was told would be contacted and expected to visit the Exhibition on Opening Night never materialised, which was hugely disappointing. It was literally my own invites who came, so I had masses of food left which had cost a bomb, but went to the refuge for the homeless, so it didn't go to waste. The wine not drunk I was able to return to the wholesaler and got a refund for.

The art scene here is vibrant and promising with Galleries popping up regularly and some older stalwarts leading the way with stables of local and quite well known artists selling for high prices, as the Maltese, who tend to be the wealthier aspect of the population, come over to attend the Private Views of their favourite artists. Their tastes however are often for religious depictions and detailed realism which my work is most certainly not. After getting to know some other Gozo Expat artists, I am realising that it is not possible to make a living from sales of work here, any more than it was in the UK, which is rather depressing. There is a lot of competition and the Gozitan's don't usually buy art. My own friends and acquaintances have been very supportive and enthusiastic about my work and many have bought from me, but it's not enough to be profitable. I need to find something else to earn me enough money to live on. I need to get a job. Thankfully this is possible in this country and since I'm capable of working for an Accountant because I know how to use Sage, I find some part-time work in the Village which is extremely convenient. Salaries here however are exceedingly low – below the minimum wage in the UK, so this was just about enough to pay for my monthly food bill, but not much else, though thankfully I was still receiving some income from my involvement in the UK business I left behind in 2016.

12th February, 2019

After attending a women's group that get together for philosophical chats in the evening once a month, held at local Astrologer Penny's house, my life changed and took a new direction. Penny Dix knows her stuff and she kindly provided me with an astrological reading, based on my date and time of birth. It was all very interesting, but what Penny also actually did was very kindly and subtly give me the kick up the backside I needed to get out in the World and find something to do that would support me. I took her welcome advice and I've enrolled in a TESOL teaching course, with a view to being able to teach online all over the World without having to leave home or Hamish for any part of the day. It was hard work, took me four months to complete, but it has literally later down the line stopped me from being extremely hungry and living in a field!

28th July, 2019

I am now a qualified TESOL English teacher, which is a little scary. I start trolling the internet to find a Teaching Platform that will provide me with willing students and lesson plans to work with and hopefully a decent hourly rate of pay. This takes quite some time as many of these teaching sites require their teachers to have a Degree as well as a TESOL Certificate. For the time being I continue entering invoices onto Sage and Excel three mornings a week, but Hamish and I are nearly dying in the heat of this tiny and very closed in flat.

4th September, 2019

I've now decided to abandon my diary.   I will come back to this book at some point later in my life here, but as far as the diary goes, this is the last entry and it feels the right moment to abandon it as I'm about to start teaching and won't really have the time.

ABOUT SOME OF THE VILLAGES

Xaghra

This is the village I first decided to live in when I arrived in 2016 and moved back to in 2020. The square is a hive of activity in summer and there are a variety of restaurants and a couple of Bars – Rubbles Bar being the best in my opinion for quality and amount of wine served for the best price. There are other restaurants away from the square, including a Chinese, but I never went to it. The village sits above the best long sandy beach on the island, called Ramla Bay. It is also home to the Gigantia Temple – one of the main tourist attractions on the island and certainly well worth a visit. The museum is very interesting and the temple remains are exceedingly ancient, full of mystery and depiction of the Divine Feminine of our ancient past.

There are a few small supermarkets and other shops too. Also a petrol station, butchers, a branch of the Bank of Valletta, a library, post office and also a global ATM. It's a large sprawling village with some wonderful views in some areas and quiet little lanes in others. It has a great countryside short walk with views over Victoria that takes you past the remains of an ancient stone temple, now used as a seat for dog walkers to stop and have a chat. There are lots of Brits who live in Xaghra, I suppose because you can basically get most of whatever you need there without having to go to Victoria. It also has a very steep winding hill that is a back road down to Victoria which only takes five minutes by car. Xaghra is in the middle of Gozo, directly north of Victoria which is the Capital.

Gharb

Gharb is perhaps the most picturesque of all the villages, mostly because it has the largest number of traditional old Maltese houses which are far more beautiful inside than they are outside, but with this in mind, the old houses on the outside do have far more character and charm than the modern flat constructions the Maltese and Gozitan's seem to be obsessed with. On the outskirts of Gharb you have Ta'Pinu, the most amazing church on the island, built to replace a tiny rural church where an Gharb resident heard the voice of the Virgin Mary. There is a delightful museum on the left just as you approach the village which was the house the woman who heard the voice lived in and everyone should visit the Museum before they see the magnificent Ta'Pinu because it will make the church visit much more relevant.

Gharb is delightful and has a tranquility that kicks in as soon as you get to the Viaduct and leave the bustle behind. It too, has its busy times, as do all the towns and villages. My end of Gharb was very quiet and you could hear a pin drop most of the night, at least when the dogs weren't barking, or when noisy weekend visitors weren't still partying at 3:00 a.m.! The whole village goes to sleep. 'Rush hour' in Gharb, in as much as it could be called, was just more cars than normal, but enough to certainly put me off having a cat that had to cross them in its territory. Yet once everyone's home, it settles right down and is so peaceful, once all the tourists have departed.

You have to travel through Gharb and San Lawrence to get to Djwera – the inland sea and an area that used to be known as the Azure Window.

There's also a back road down to the coast with amazing coastal walks that can eventually take you to the Salt Pans and Marsalforn. There are some really good restaurants in Gharb, but they are a bit pricey, yet the food is very good: Grazie Mille – obviously Italian and Salvina's were my favourites. I do have to mention the Gharb Rangers Pub and restaurant though and the indomitable Dave and his Vapour Clouds. The Rangers was the meeting point for drinks and chats, watching the Sports and catching up with local friends and tourists. In the summer the upstairs terrace has amazing views. The food there is also acceptable for a meal out without fuss or high prices.

Gharb feels a bit more rural than many villages because it's on the far west of the island and has a great deal of land around it, so it's great for walking and very quiet at night in the Winter when there are no noisy tourists or loud visitors from that other island!

Zebugg

This village, pronounced Zeboodge, is the highest one on the island and it has the best views. It's a sleepy little village though with not much going on. They do have the best little restaurant for Pizza on the whole island, called Francesco's, as well as a couple of other restaurants. This village is the coldest in winter because it's so high up, but also the coolest in summer. There are great walks around the outskirts of the village and it's a very short drive down to the incredible Salt Pans, the beach of Xwejni Bay and then on to Obajjar and in to Marsalforn. Zebugg is a bit like Marmite though – you either love it or hate it.

Marsalforn

Marsalforn is a bit like the 'Bournemouth' of Gozo. Right on the sea front with a small beach, a few hotels, and a plethora of restaurants all pleading with you to try their wares. There are bars, restaurants, cafes, shops, places to swim, hang out and enjoy the atmosphere of frequent live music, people watching and generally chilling out. I always quite liked visiting Marsalforn, but I'd never want to live there. Bearing in mind I did for three months, in the winter it was great, in the summer, it's like Blackpool and to be avoided unless you like crowds. It is however the place where most of the immigrant workers live so the housing quality there is often poor, though there are some lovely spots. It has some great restaurants though, right on the water's edge and you can walk along the seafront to places like Otters Restaurant, being careful not to disturb or tread on the fishing nets spread out by the fishermen after a working day. It has huge charm and a wonderful people watching atmosphere and you will always find someone to talk to. I rather liked it for the three winter months I was living there, whilst searching for the house I eventually found in Gharb, but it gets terribly crowded in the high season. Electra is the Pub/Restaurant for locals to congregate in during the winter months and the food there is good for a general kind of meal. The Glassbox – a small Pub run by a Brit called Gary, hosts live music frequently and is a small friendly place, but for my palette, he needs to improve his wine selection!

The Salt Pans on the western edge of the town are a favourite walking place for many, as the road is a quiet one and takes you along the edge of the sea with the patterned squares of the salt collectors between you and the ocean. Salt has been faithfully collected here for hundreds of years and just as you commence your walk along the concrete road, you can find the Salt Seller, offering small bags of the most delicious salt for very little money. The Salt is piled into heaps to dry out and this ancient art is both a pleasure to watch and an even better one to taste.

Nadur

Nadur is a village that feels like a favourite coat. It's long, widespread, has some of the best village views in some areas of it and it hosts probably the biggest social event on the island once a year which is the Carnival. The Maltese flock to the island for this event – every accommodation in the village and surrounding area is booked and locals cash in on hiring out spare bedrooms. Every type of dressing up you could imagine is flaunted shamelessly and behaviour is rather too much for most of us living on the reserved island of Gozo, whether local or expat. The noise is deafening far beyond Nadur, but it only lasts about 3 days and then they all bugger off back home. On a more conservative note is the wine festival which brings in a more discerning type of drinker.

Nadur has a variety of shops, a great little supermarket, post office, two banks, restaurants and the beaches of San Blas and Dahlet Qorrot. It also hosts the hotel catering College and a visit is essential during the term times of the College where sampling the menu for about €8.00 per person one can munch through the delights of future Chefs and enjoy new and upcoming dishes in the future of cuisine. For many however, Nadur is a bit of another Marmite village, but I always liked it, though I never lived there.

Xlendi

This little village tucked down on the south coast is a tourist hotspot. It has a small beach and harbour with restaurants dotted along the waterfront. Some are very good, others not so much. On first inspection, it looks rather shabby and parking anytime from early May to the end of October is a nightmare. It's a village that you feel could really pick itself up because it has an ideal outlook, yet somehow it remains stubbornly shabby chic and living there in the summer must be hellish - nowhere to park your car and your village inundated by tourists. Not a great place to live unless you really enjoy vibrant crowds and people watching and parking hundreds of yards away from your flat. There are very few old houses here. Living accommodation is mostly new apartment blocks. The walk along the left side of the bay and out beyond the village was lovely, but I rarely went to Xlendi.

Sannat

Home to one of the best hairdresser's on the island as I discovered far too late. Also home to the Ta'Çenc hotel, one of the best on the island. There are incredible cliff walks to be had in Sannat and also the Il'Kanta restaurant belonging to Ta'Cenc – a restaurant overlooking the sea with a great menu, though sometimes a varying quality of service. Sannat, like Gharb has a large number of old houses, some of which are amazing. There are a couple of places to eat, but generally Sannat is a village to live in and walk about, especially if you have dogs, but there's not much else to do. There is a bank, but the village is only five minutes to Victoria so you can do and get everything there.

Qala

Now this village I have left until last for a very good reason. As you will have read in the diary part, this is a village of party animals who are mostly on the outside of normality. Eccentrics all, a mix of locals and expats all jumbled into each other, most of whom are living their lives entirely based around a famous bar called Zeppi's, owned and run by a delightfully wacky woman called Sonia. Zeppi's, is opened at about 7:30 a.m. most mornings, by the indomitable Gary and the Gozitan's congregate for coffee, a doughnut and conversation to start off the day. As the morning wares on into elevenses or noonies, the regular drinkers would arrive – mostly Expats - 11:30 a.m. being an acceptable time for the first alcohol of the day! Thankfully I usually preferred it to be a bit later.

Zeppi's is rather an icon in time and will always be remembered as that place where people who have left this dimension, are still talked about. Dear Alex, once long ago married to Sonia and the two of them sharing the love and responsibility of their dog Zappa. Zappa freely wandered the roads of Qala, making his way between home and the pub to find his Mom or Dad somewhere and if he couldn't find them, he'd just lie in the road and all cars came to a stop because of the Zappa obstacle. I have never known a dog have such respect, but I guess that's what happens when you're named after Frank Zappa!

The live bands that played at Zeppi's on a Friday or Saturday night were always crowd pleasers, but Sonia is an astute business woman and she had her Maltese band evenings and her local/expat evenings and each Saturday night would be packed. A bit rough if you lived right next door to the pub. The street in front of the pub would be heaving with people, the road closed, everyone enjoying the sounds without having to be inside. Having this kind of pub on my doorstep was a big issue for my drinking. I mean I could just crawl home as I lived right across the square from the pub. I did however meet a great many people, as I loved listening to live music and was quite happy getting to the pub a little bit early, finding a seat indoors with Hamish, reading my Kindle and just waiting for things to start up. I talked to a great many people, mostly from Malta in the early days before I met those crazy locals and I loved every moment of my Saturday nights.

So apart from Zeppi's, Qala has Hondoq Bay – a beautiful beach tucked down out of the wind, boat hire to the turquoise waters of Comino, a fantastic restaurant serving great food, windsurfing, kayaks, a doggie swimming place and a coastal walk to Mgarr. There is also a great walk at the top coastal end of the village along a paved road, between the Riding Stables and the Quarry where views of Sicily and erupting Etna can be viewed on clear days.

Qala has lots to offer, three small supermarkets, a great pharmacy and it's only five minutes away from the Ferry Port. The other most notable mention is Xerri l-Bukkett – a kind of sports club/restaurant that does have the most spectacular view in all of Gozo. Their food is very good, their wine pleasing and cheap and I spent many a late afternoon there admiring the view across to the turquoise sea of Comino and beyond to Malta, whilst absorbing great Gozo hospitality. It was my favourite place to go whilst I lived in Qala because sometimes I just liked to sit and read my kindle in peace and quiet.

There are a number of very good restaurants in Qala – the D-Bar, Ta'Vestru and several other new ones. This village is the most social one on the island and the mix of both local and expat seems to work here more than any other village. One expat friend I made described it as the village of alternative thinkers, the slightly outcast of modern society and on reflection I would have to agree with you ma Cherie! I was most certainly drinking too much there, so if you are trying to cut down or cut out your drinking habit, DON'T go to Qala! The inhabitants for the most part are an eclectic mix of winos, however amusing and entertaining they may be! The initials J R come to mind. You old rogue!

I have not covered all of the villages – there is still Munxar, Ghjanseilem, Mgarr, Xewkia, Ghasri, and heaven forbid if I've forgotten any, but these villages were visited less by me and so I'm not talking about them all. Mgarr, the island Port I loved for a while, but in mid-2019 they started a rather horrendous excavation for profitability and totally destroyed the old harbour to apparently make way for the docking of superyachts. Oh dear, yet more of a sad decision based on the profit of now, rather than the future sustainability of tourists wanting to visit a unique island that still lives in the old way of life.

AFTER FOUR YEARS OF LIFE IN GOZO - 2020

I really haven't spent much time in Malta in the four years I've been here. There is lots going on there – a vibrant scene of all you could want, yet the traffic problems, having no sat nav or phone GPS, together with the heat in summer mean that actually I spend far too much time in Gozo, which can get very claustrophobic if you don't get off the island for a day or so, at least six times a year. Yet the frenetic traffic, lack of signage and the fear of getting lost prevent me from getting off Gozo as much as I should in order to have a more contented life. There was once a ferry service from Gozo direct to Valletta and it would be so much better for everyone if they reinstated this service, even if it was only a couple of times a week. I would have used it regularly and it may have changed my mind about the decision I made in August this year.

Since initially writing this, I understand that the fast ferry to Valletta is now operational again, as of 2021, which will make life so much better for everyone. What a shame I missed this fantastic service, which apparently runs daily.

Malta is a much larger island than Gozo and it's vibrant, busy, and cosmopolitan with some beautiful areas. Valletta is superb and there's lots to see and do. I think my biggest mistake living in Gozo was that I just didn't explore Malta enough, but the bigger island is like a huge city with large green areas and I'm not a fan of cities for any length of time.

The Gozitan people are delightful, particularly the older population, but the younger ones can be exceedingly quick to anger if you have an issue they disagree with, or heaven forbid, if you criticise something. That Mediterranean temperament exists here in all its glory. The expat population of Brits is large and they are a good bunch of people, some having lived on the island since time began. There are Expats from everywhere and they are interesting, come from a mixture of countries and cultures, are eclectic, kind and highly social, but naturally gossip does occur because it's a small island and everyone knows someone who knows so and so. Rumour spreads like wildfire and often it's untrue because you're hearing news that has been passed on and embellished numerous times. Yet as is the way with gossip, people forget the last story because there is a newer one to discuss and pass on. Not everyone does this of course, but unfortunately it's inevitable on a small island, that some in the population will be gleeful to pass on bits of information about others that are titillating to their audience.

The island has changed quite dramatically in the four years I've been here. Cranes have appeared in many of the villages as more and more apartment buildings occupy the previously wild green spaces that were overgrown by Prickly Pear cactus and inhabited by feral cats. It seems as if the construction industry is determined to occupy every available space in every village. Sadly the old stone houses are often demolished to make way for the modern apartment blocks and the old stone houses are so much better at insulating the heat of summer and the cold of winter. Each time another is demolished, a little bit more of the old culture and way of life is lost forever. The young Maltese and Gozitan's don't like old houses and want to live in brand new apartments. Perhaps the saddest part of all this frenetic construction is that many buildings are only shell built and can sit unfinished for years. I have to ask myself why? It's certainly not good for the island which is supposed to be the jewel in Malta's crown in terms of quiet rural idyllic life. It has certainly changed since Google Earth last updated their image of it which must be at least fifteen years old.

In four years Malta too has undergone further huge amounts of construction and I found numerous Maltese telling me that they felt the Government had allowed their island to be ruined because of too much building work and traffic over the last twenty years. Many of the Maltese feel this way and although they would not want to live in Gozo, over the four year period of being here, it became more and more evident that the island was being swelled by Maltese every weekend, escaping the hustle and bustle, traffic, fumes and stress of Malta. More and more houses and land were being taken up and built to accommodate Maltese who want a weekend getaway. This naturally put far more stress on Gozo and its inhabitants who found Victoria an impossibility on a Saturday because of traffic mayhem. Restaurants and local haunts packed with Maltese long after the summer tourists stopped arriving. If the weather was good Gozo would be inundated with Maltese, often until the end of November, the last moment of opening for most of the restaurants and well beyond the tourist season.

For the first couple of years I found the island to be very quiet from mid-October until about mid-May. Because of the great walks on Gozo and the Autumn/Spring weather, there would always be a few tourists around in late October and then those intrepid ones that would start to arrive in early April, but generally the island was very quiet until the influx of our larger island brothers and sisters who extended the season somewhat and often also come for Christmas and New Year. This has not been good for the residents of Gozo, in terms of the peace and tranquility that has always been greatly required to recuperate from the busy and long summer season.

The other thing that gets up the nose of all the local residents is that the Maltese often have no respect for the locals who live full time in the area they've chosen for their 'holiday home'. Local farmers often rise at 5:00 a.m. to start work and don't take kindly to loud music being played into the wee hours, or to the Maltese's dogs who are on a visit away from home and bark for most of the night. It's no wonder there's a little resentment between the inhabitants of the two islands. The Expats soon learned to side with the Gozitan's over any arguments and who could blame them? Expats don't like loud music in the wee hours or stressed out barking dogs either.

The disillusionment of Gozo for me actually started to happen towards the middle of 2018. I was, to be fair, getting bored in Gharb because it's not really the place to live alone. It got very lonely and although I had a few married friends in the village and knew as drinking buddies a few locals and Expats at the Gharb Rangers Club, it wasn't the sort of place for a woman on her own to hang about in on a very regular basis. There was nowhere else to socialize though. My old small farmhouse was delightful – cool in the summer and warm in winter, but the rent was on the high side at €600 a month and the landlord was going to increase it in March, 2019 and a personal change in finances meant even the current rent was too expensive. I decided after eighteen months to move once again.

Through someone I knew, I found a very cheap, though rather unsuitable flat on the church square in Qala. The suitability of the cheap €320 a month rent, allowed me for a while, to overlook the unsuitable. I moved in during late October, 2018. The move to this village gave me the boost I needed and restored my faith in the island. Qala meant a much more active social life, new acquaintances and drinking buddies, so I passed that sixteen months in a daze of wine and forgotten conversations. However, after the initial summer in this flat, the unsuitable soon overcame the cheap rent. It was horrendous being on the top floor with the sun beating down on my ceilings all day, which heated them like a radiator, still on warp factor four at midnight. I nearly died, as did my dog. Living on the church square ANYWHERE in Gozo means you will be subjected to church bells ringing all night long on the hour, on the half hour, for ages during the day and just about every moment there is. Be warned, don't live within 800 metres of a church!

I realised after four summers in Gozo, that I really was not enjoying the weather from the end of May to the end of September. Believe me, it is relentless heat and humidity, with dust and hardly a drop of rain. The flat was like an oven for four months and a freezer for two! I knew I had to leave it and even contemplated going back to the UK in early 2020. I didn't really want to do that though, despite the fact that I was not enjoying Gozo as much as I had hoped I would when I arrived. However I knew I had to get out of this flat and actually get out of Qala. I decided to go flat hunting and by this time, my finances had got better and I could afford €500 a month in rent.

I found a really super flat in Xaghra and I got really excited about going back to village I started my Gozitan life in. I hoped it would put everything right again with my relationship to Gozo. The flat was airy, bright and high up, so I imagined cool breezes blowing through and because it was mid-floor, I knew it wouldn't be as hot in summer, nor as cold in winter, but this naivety was short lived really. I moved at the end of February, 2020, just before Covid lockdowns kicked off. Those initial three months of March, April and May, 2020 were very scary, extremely lonely and basically total shite. During the three months of the initial lockdown I, like everyone else, had a great deal of time alone to think.

The European lifestyle really appealed to me, but I didn't account for the extreme heat here – quite often up to 37 degrees and after four years, I really just couldn't cope with it anymore. It was relentless and debilitating and prevented any kind of normal life for four months of the year. I did the math. Four months of extreme heat, two months of uncomfortable cold which equalled six months of weather I hated. WTF? This was NOT part of the dream I had whilst packing up and selling off large amounts of my stuff back in Somerset. There are not many flats in the lower rental scope of €400 to €600 a month which have air con and without it life is just intolerable. I don't really like living in air conditioning anyway, but there are times when it's essential. I hate the summer, Hamish hates the summer - just about all of us hate that heat. It's always a welcome change to everyone when it rains here and I never ever thought I would say after living in North Devon for twenty years, I would miss the rain!

January is totally freezing. 90% of the houses or flats on the market do not have any kind of central heating. Most of us moderate income people rely on propane gas cylinders for our ovens and heat. It's certainly the most economical with a small cylinder costing €16 and lasting ten to fourteen days in the coldest of winter. I have learned that you need a DeLongue gas heater with the blue flame. This costs more, but compared to the €65 heaters you get at the ironmongers like DOM, Caruana or other electrical/gas suppliers, it's a zillion times better as a heater, without all the issues of the cheap ones. Besides a great heater you will need a good supply of thermal vests and thick wool socks. It is flipping freezing here in January and sometimes February too. It often feels colder indoors than out. It is not a dry crispy, sunny, frosty cold – oh no, it's a driving north west wind, heavy rain pounding you, 70% humidity and it feels like the opposite end of the spectrum to an early August day, yet equally unwelcome and equally unpleasant.

On a more positive note, there are things to do, but they quite often cost money and I was not in a position to afford most of them. I am going to talk about pre-virus, because since then the whole bloody World has changed! There are lots of boating things and water sports. You can take a boat trip to see the Shearwater birds at Sunset, courtesy of Birdlife Malta. Well worth the fifteen euro cost that the trip charges, departing from Mgarr. The island is great for scuba diving, with many clubs and opportunities to learn. There's a man who does Exciting Hikes and takes you on walks through areas of Gozo you would never otherwise find or see. You can find him on Meetup, together with things like Yoga on the beach, Zumba at Hondoq and Gozo scientific café, holding regular very interesting talks. There are Art Galleries and lots of private viewings. There are choirs to join, Spiritual retreat evenings, theatre, writing groups, Festas, horse racing, recitals, fireworks, concerts and small live bands playing regularly somewhere.

There is a superb annual wine festival under the stars at Ramla in August each year, put on by the Marsovin Vineyard. Vini'de Caprisi puts on a gastronomic night under the stars on the Salt Pans and for a vast sum you can dress in white and eat and drink quality, whilst hopefully making new friends. I have always wanted to go to one of these but shudder at the €150 price tag! I have however been to two of the Marsovin Vineyard 'Do's', both were amazing because they get a really good local band to play and everyone dances the night away. I always felt right at home because everyone gets totally tick-like! It's a boomer night for taxis.

Of course there are all the restaurants and bars/drinking holes and naturally in this heat and with nothing more pressing to do, you catch up with friends and get into your cups somewhat. They are not _all_ that strict here about the drink driving thing. Scarily it's rather the same in Malta (and they drive fast there!) At least here in Gozo you don't usually see anyone doing over 65 km per hour and most people do about 50, so that's about 30 miles per hour. I'm not suggesting you get into a car and drive unless you're capable, but they don't check your alcohol limit unless you give them a reason to. You do sometimes see some old boy in his ancient pick up weaving all over the road and know he's had a skinful, but he will be doing about 15 mph and usually finds his way home without harm to himself or others.

For me though, despite these social things that one can do, I still feel bereft of the inspiration to my soul and spirit. I need nature and countryside and getting away from humanity. That is very difficult here as rubbish is frequently dumped anywhere. This is not a tidy island and the countryside is often scattered with rubbish and small sandstone hides from which to shoot any living thing that flies. Yeah, they shoot song birds here, they shoot ANY bird at all that happens to be flying in front of their guns. They shoot Robins, Finches, Blackbirds and Thrushes, as well as larger birds of prey. Those who like birds and don't shoot, often trap wild birds with the help of those enslaved the season before, put into a 6 inch wire cage, with water, but often no shade, expecting them to call their brothers-in-arms into the lure of the waiting net. Once caught, they are caged forever, if they're lucky, into a reasonable sized Aviary, others into small cages, singing for their supper. It is the worst thing about the country and many local people feel the same. Birdlife Malta are doing all they can to stop this destruction of the bird life in Malta & Gozo, but they beat a drum onto deaf ears most of the time. Consequently you rarely hear birdsong.

I still think that the biggest threat facing the peaceful rural idyll of Gozo is the influx of the Maltese, who are seeking weekend homes here. The increase in building work and house prices in the four years

I've been here are considerable and inevitably traffic in Victoria is often an issue. There are cranes everywhere and building work happening on just about every village spare plot.

I've spoken to a great many Maltese, particularly at Zeppi's. They admit that their Governments have ruined Malta, so now they come to Gozo to escape, but they don't realise that by them all feeling this way, they will make Gozo into a mini-Malta. When I came here Gozo was in its last throes of being the smaller, quieter, uncool (as far as the Maltese were concerned) and insignificant relation of Malta, to the place where the Maltese now want to come and escape their busy, overcrowded and traffic laden home. The population of Malta is nearly half a million, whilst the population of Gozo is about 38,000 – a manageable number who live here in peace and quiet in the winter, but whose numbers swell to unacceptable levels with weekend visits and general tourism.

I wondered back in 2016 when I left my country of birth what I would miss the least about England? Would it be Health and Safety and the "Nanny State", both of which are non-existent here – no I certainly never missed those! There is danger everywhere here; cliff tops without safety rails, dodgy steps with uneven surfaces, pavements with multiple trip hazards, holes in the road – you name it, there are ways to die here! Do people die? Not usually unless they're very old, ill, or go swimming when the sea is too rough. They expect adults to be responsible enough to look after themselves and their children, which they do, exceedingly well. Children here are generally well behaved, active outdoors, slender, healthy and learn from an early age not to walk over cliffs, or disappear down pot holes not surrounded by red and white plastic fences. All the children grow up bilingual and in fact English is so ingrained into the Maltese language that even when talking to each other, the locals switch between Maltese and English without even noticing. This makes these islands ideal for Brits not wanting to learn a new language. The Maltese also adore the British and welcome them with open arms.

So, you probably gather by now that, although I hated the British weather, I also find that the complete extreme from British weather here on this Mediterranean island does not suit me either - one of the major reasons for wanting to leave. The other issues are more complex. Gozo has changed so much while I've been here and many of the islanders, expat or local would agree with me. Everyone fears Gozo becoming a miniature Malta, but I and quite a few friends feel that it already has. A number of British couples I know have already left. Certainly the island and lifestyle will go on attracting those Brits looking for something other than the cold, grey, wet land of cake and corruption, but if you're going to do this, you need to do it soon, before the Gozo so many Brits have adored for years, will be spoiled forever. Too many cranes on the small island horizon, too many small spaces of wilderness tucked between the houses in villages, now being developed and turned into three or four storey flats. Prickly pears and distant cats obliterated with the sound of excavators digging foundations for yet more empty shells of buildings, perhaps never to be inhabited, until distant cats and prickly pears take up residence once again in a jungle of stone that once was called nature.

If you are part of a couple and want to find a less stressful, mostly peaceful life on a small Mediterranean island - perhaps you want to retire, or just work from home, enjoy drinking and eating out and meeting new people, Gozo will be ideal if you don't mind the fact that it gets so hot you literally melt for four months of the year. It's also an economical place to live and your money will go much further here than in England.

So I do recommend this delightful island for those who don't mind the heat, or can afford air conditioning, especially if you're not into the scenery of nature in its glory and are happy with some great, though not spectacular views. This little Mediterranean island is great for swimming because the Med is so warm from the end of June to early November and there are some lovely beaches and secluded spots to find. This is also a very safe and trusting place to live. I never bothered to lock my car, or even roll up the windows and once by accident I left my Kindle on the front seat with the window open. It was still there when I got back. A woman on her own is quite safe on this gem of an island.

Ever since I have been here there has been a deep longing for the countryside and the nature of England and it just does not exist here. Sure you can find lovely places with great views and no one around you and I've really appreciated these things, but it's not the lush green of lots of rain, trees, flowers and water. It's not got the wildness of a natural environmental spirit connection that I need and desperately crave. Spring and the yellow flowers are wonderful, as is the brief lushness of the landscape, but it is both short lived and most certainly lacks both diversity and the true beauty and variance of Nature's pallet in the right climatic conditions.

Although I loved being back in Xaghra and enjoyed the social side of the Square and the walks around the village, I was getting restless and it was getting very hot again. My new flat was much cooler than the Qala flat, but I knew that once June arrived, I would be a prisoner indoors once again, unable to be outside after 7:30 a.m. until it cooled down enough to walk Hamish twelve hours later. I was getting very down in the dumps about the lockdown of a virus and the lockup of the heat. I also realised after the lockdown period of three months, that I had a lot of acquaintances in Gozo, but had actually only made a few true friends. I came to the conclusion that I should not make any decision to stay on a small island I was now disillusioned with because of my social life. The reality of it was that I knew lots of people, but they were not enough of a reason to stay.

I had taken out a six month tenancy on the flat in Xaghra and it was in late July, 2020 that I decided Gozo and I had to part ways. I enjoyed my four years, two months living here, but found the smallness of the island constricting and the option to leave it for trips to Malta, unappealing. I also missed the birdsong of England and the lushness of vegetation, varying scenery and all things that grow in areas with an abundance of rain.

Am I going back to England? Am I heck! I can't stand the weather there either. Nor a lot of other things, particularly now! I'm looking for mysterious fogs and ethereal mists brought in by the Atlantic and the mountains. Somewhere atmospheric after this endless searing white sky of summer, debilitating heat and sun since early June. It gets so utterly tedious and I know Hamish feels the same way.

It was time to pray again. Initially, before I decided what rock to hop onto next, I had questioned why God had brought me here to this country and this small little gem of an island that I had enjoyed for the most part, yet now felt miserable and depressed. Then it dawned on me. Certainly, I would never have met Hamish, but also if I hadn't come here, I would never have found out about my new rock. I would never have had the courage to move to my latest rock directly from England because it would have felt too foreign for me then. I now see that the transition time I had in a foreign country that was so aligned with the UK gave me the courage to make another hop. Back in 2016, Malta felt manageable and achievable to me when I first decided to emigrate. I could do this.

There are language issues on my new rock and it's very un-British. Back in 2016, this rock was not even on my radar of knowledge and would have felt far too daunting to move to. I didn't know at the time of being directed to Malta and Gozo, that there were greater plans afoot for me which meant a four year stint somewhere I could gain my confidence. Neither could I possibly comprehend in my future, that a man I met on Gozo, whom I thought was a friend, who turned out not to be, would direct me to where I really needed to be.

I think I may now have finished my Rock Hopping, have finally found somewhere I will be happy and where the climate suits me. Yes, I feel a little bit like Goldilocks, but hey, she got it right in the end didn't she?

And .... No I'm not telling you where it is right now. You'll just have to wait for the next instalment from the tales of a Rock Hopping Single Granny!

Printed in Great Britain
by Amazon

77292789R00068